THE CRISIS INTERVENTION MANUAL

3rd Edition

KURT CHRISTIANSEN, PSY.D.

Published by:
Empathy Works
2118 Wilshire Blvd. Ste. 843, Santa Monica, CA 90403

www.EmpathyWorks.net

ISBN: 978-0-9994228-1-6

"Exercises in the Perception of Feelings" from *Improving Therapeutic Communication,* copyright 2002 by D. Corydon Hammond, reprinted with permission of John Wiley & Sons, Inc.

TABLE OF CONTENTS

> *"Never believe that a few caring people can't change the world, for, indeed, that's all who ever have."*
>
> Margaret Mead

INTRODUCTION

"To be listened to is . . . a nearly unique experience for
most people. Man clamors for the freedom to express
himself and for knowing that he counts." –Robert C. Murphy

The mission of this manual is to educate you on how to help, support, and empower people, with the specific focus on assisting callers on a Helpline.

Empathy is the primary ingredient to helping people. The ability to understand, accept, and show care for people is the essence of empathy.

You will learn how our judgments and limiting beliefs are our greatest *barriers* to developing empathy, and that listening, clear and honest communication, and increasing awareness of self and others are the *openings* to empathy.

The following is covered in this manual:

- Active listening skills and techniques of clear communication.
- Information and specific examples for how to handle a myriad of different calls.
- Theories on why certain individual and social problems occur.
- Suggestions towards prevention of these problems.
- Resources and referrals for how to get help for self and others.
- Practical exercises designed to develop empathy and release negative judgments.

"Every time one person resolves one issue the whole
of humanity moves forward." –H. Ronald Hulnick

More than likely you will be touched or triggered by at least a few of the topics in this book. Use everything you feel and experience for your own healing and growth. Your effectiveness as a listener, helper, or counselor depends on it. It takes both inner *and* outer work to facilitate change, so you are encouraged to make full use of the exercises in this book. As you do, you may discover that not only are you a more effective crisis worker, but a more loving, compassionate, and peaceful person in your day-to day-life.

"Be the change you wish to see in the world." –Gandhi

THE BASIC TECHNIQUES

"The first duty of love is to listen."
—Paul Tillich

OPENING THE CALL

Most of the anxiety we feel about taking calls on a crisis line occurs before picking up the phone. So let's take a deep breath, bring forward a little courage, and jump right in.

The phone *rings*.

When you answer the phone, keep your *greeting* simple, professional, and warm. Be genuine, open, and ready to help. Sounding bored, annoyed, or overly happy are not the most effective ways to greet a caller.

<u>Get their name and age</u> as soon as you can. You want to get to know who you are speaking with. People like hearing their name, and it makes the call much more personable than referring to them as sir, ma'am, you, dude, or man.

What if the caller does not want to give their name or age?

If they do not want to give their name, you can ask if there is something you could call them . . . a nickname perhaps? If not, do not push the subject. Just move on and open the conversation: *"What's going on tonight?"*

The same goes for age. If they do not want to give it, do not push it. Just use your intuition the best you can as you gather more information.

What if the caller wants to speak to someone else?

The rule for most crisis helplines is *we never hand off the phone*.
If the person asks:

> *"Is there a woman there I can speak with?"*
> *"Someone older?"*
> *"Is Harriet there? I spoke to her last week."*

A suggested response is . . .

> *"Not right now, but **I'm** here to listen. What's going on? What's your name?"*
> Engage the caller right away in the conversation, letting them know you want to help. Once you pick up that phone, the call is yours.

Is this call confidential?

There will be instances when people will want to know if the call is confidential. Yes, it is. State it as if it were a rule, which it is. *We are a confidential line.* This can help you gain some trust from a caller who is hesitant about revealing personal information to a stranger.

> *"Yes this is confidential. It's just between you and me."*

Do not let them think about it too long. Open up the immediate opportunity to talk.

We may also have to explain the purpose of the crisis line. What we do and who it is for. Give the person time to ask questions if they choose to. Do not rush them.

There are certain instances when we are mandated to break confidentiality. Please consult your organization about these specifics.

Openers

When beginning a call, use broad openings like:

> *"What's going on tonight?"*
> *"What can I help you with?"*
> *"What would you like to talk about tonight?"*

These kind of openers make it clear that the caller is to take the lead. For the caller who is hesitant or uncertain about what to do, these openings can stimulate them to take the initiative. The listener should avoid the conventional pleasantries and refrain from making small talk.

SAFETY

Before we go any further, **safety** must be mentioned. On a crisis helpline, there are going to be instances when a person's safety is in jeopardy. We must keep this in the back of our mind during all calls. It will not always be apparent, so when you get a gut feeling or an indication from a caller that they or someone else might be in danger, you must ask. *Never hesitate to ask about a caller's safety.* More about this will be discussed in later sections.

Needs of the caller

In order to assist a caller, we first have to determine what they need help with. Why have they called? People call for all sorts of reasons: information, referrals, to vent, crisis intervention (violence, overdose, suicide, etc.), emotional support, concern for another, just to name a few.

Some people know what they need and others do not. Many callers are in emotional distress or feel confused and don't know what to do. We are here to help them figure it out, and in order to do that we must gather the **Big Picture** and acquire all the necessary information.

Big Picture

To determine what a caller needs, we must first gather information. Information about their situation, their feelings, and their motives. Always remember to ask about their feelings. *Feelings are the most important part of the information.* This is the primary reason most people call a helpline – bottled up, unresolved, conflicted, and overwhelming emotions.

When gathering information, be aware of making any assumptions or premature conclusions. Example:

Caller: *"My Grandma died yesterday."*

Ineffective response: *"That must be hard for you. You need to grieve. Here's the number for a counselor."*

Effective responses: *"How do you feel about that? How are you feeling?"*

Caller: *"Kind of relieved. Is that bad?"*

The latter response takes the call in an entirely different direction and refrains from making any assumptions about the caller's perspective and feelings. Make sure to gather all information with openness and curiosity.

Trust

> *"No soul is desolate as long as there is a human being*
> *for whom it can feel trust and reverence." –T.S. Eliot*

The majority of callers are not just going to open up to you and tell you their deepest darkest secrets. They may feel uncomfortable telling a stranger certain things they feel ashamed about. So in order for us to get the Big Picture we must first gain their trust.

Trusting comes from the belief that it is safe for them to be open and vulnerable with us, and that we will embrace and accept *whatever they tell us.*

So how do we gain a caller's trust?

Rapport

> *"The best rapport arises not out of some direct effort to get along*
> *well with the caller, but out of a simple and sincere effort to listen and*
> *hear accurately what he or she has to say." –Andrew LeCompte*

Rapport is a relationship between caller and listener. A *good* rapport has a harmonious, give and take to the conversation that often opens the door for trust and disclosure. You know when there is good rapport when you enjoy talking to each other and there is an easy flow to the conversation.

How do we gain rapport with a caller? How do we get people to trust and open up to us?

Empathy

> *"Empathic listening involves entering another person's*
> *world non-judgmentally and accepting their feelings*
> *and meanings." –On Becoming a Counselor*

The most effective way to gain trust and develop a strong rapport is by being empathic. Empathy is an understanding – **an understanding of a person's situation, feelings, meanings, and motives.** We are putting ourselves in their shoes, taking another perspective, and **looking at the world through their eyes, with all of their meanings, feelings, intentions, and desires.**

True Empathy is when we recognize a person's deepest hopes and good intentions behind every word, feeling, or action. When we understand a person at the deeper levels, the door for compassion opens up. Suddenly, **we care and are concerned** about this person and we want to help them. A connection is then formed and we move into a space of unconditional acceptance. This is the essential ingredient for all change, growth, and healing. This is what most people yearn for when they call a crisis line.

Take a movie for instance. We follow the life of the character, and at first we may judge this character to be bad if they have done some "bad things." But over the course of the film, we follow their life, walk in their shoes and begin to understand why they are doing the things they do. If the movie is done effectively, we will begin to feel care for the character.

When we put ourselves in other people's shoes, we can more easily imagine that their behavior could spring from limited perception and limited awareness of options, rather than from evil intent.[1]

> *"Empathy is an intelligent, deeply respectful exploration of what lies beneath the surface of our world. It teaches us to let go of our preconceptions and enter into our relationships with open hearts and open minds." –Arthur Ciaramicoli*

Empathy is different than sympathy. Sympathy is more like pity. *"Oh, poor baby."* With sympathy we put ourselves in a position of superiority and our efforts often come across as condescending. With empathy there is a shared experience – a connection – *a recognizing of feelings inside of another that we can relate to.* We understand because we too have experienced these emotions and we know what they feel like.

Feelings are universal. All humans feel anger, sadness, fear, happiness, frustration, etc. All humans at their deepest level want the same things: peace, love, safety, freedom, connection, a sense of purpose, and we all suffer to some extent trying to attain these. The more we can recognize these emotions, desires, and needs within ourselves, the more we will notice them in others. The more we notice in others, the better we can empathize. And the better we empathize, the more effective we will be in helping others.

> *"Those wise ones who see that the consciousness within themselves is the same consciousness within all conscious beings, attain eternal peace." –Katha Upanishad*

Many people believe that we are all separate beings, running around competing for limited resources in a big game of survival of the fittest. But if that is entirely true, why do we care about others? Why does anyone help another person? Why does it feel so good, so innately right, when we help a fellow human?

> *"A Human Being is a part of the whole called by us "Universe," a part limited in time and space. He experiences himself, his thoughts, and feelings as something separated from the rest, a kind of optical delusion of consciousness. This delusion is a kind of prison for us, restricting us to our personal desires and to affection for a few persons nearest us. Our task must be to free ourselves from this prison by widening our circle of compassion to embrace all living creatures . . ." --Albert Einstein.*

We are always *whole*. A whole human being. Yet, we are also a *part* – of larger wholes – a family, society, world, and universe. This means that whatever we do to another, we do to the larger wholes. And because we are part of these wholes, what we do to another, we do to ourselves. This may be why it feels so good to help another.

Being empathic does however require a certain emotional distance. When we walk in their shoes, we are not feeling *exactly* what they are feeling, then we too may end up in an activated emotional state. Empathy is a *knowing* – a knowing of what these emotions feel like and an understanding of their experience. When someone hits their funny bone or stubs a toe, we do not feel the same pain as they do, but we know how it feels. We feel empathy for their pain. We do the same for emotions – we understand and we care.

> **"Distances in heaven are measured by degrees of empathy."**
> —*Emanuel Swedenborg*

Everyone has a unique perspective of the world, so we cannot know exactly what they are experiencing. Empathy seeks to understand their perspective by being flexible, open, curious, and objective to seeing the world in a different way – their way.

Empathy involves:

- Curiosity.
- Unconditional acceptance.
- Focusing on the present, on what is happening right now, at this very moment.
- About humility. Saying to ourselves, "My perspective is not the only one. It is partial. I have so much more to learn and experience."
- Balancing seeing others as unique individuals while finding common ground.
- Separating a person's behavior from their essence – which is love and goodness.

Empathy: The Basics

> **"Understanding a person brings us the power to love and accept him."** –*Thich Nhat Hanh*

Empathy is not just another skill that is nice to have in our counseling toolbox. Empathy is an expression of who we are. It is a complex developmental process within each of us that involves cognitive development (the taking of perspectives), emotional maturity, self-awareness, and interpersonal skills. The health and depth of *all* of our relationships depends intimately on our level of empathy.

The exercises throughout this book have been designed to assist you in deepening and developing your empathy. Take the time to work on each exercise. Building empathy takes openness, willingness, courage, patience, perseverance, and honesty. Be gentle (and empathic) with yourself as you learn a new way of seeing, being, and relating in the world.

EMPATHY DEVELOPMENT

Awareness #1

We are all doing the best we can given our circumstances and conditioning.

Whenever you feel upset with yourself or with another person, expand your awareness into the knowing that everyone is doing the best they can given what they have learned in their life. If we knew of another way, and trusted in that way, we would surely choose it.

We are all searching for greater well-being, peace, freedom, and connectedness, and in this searching and not finding, we suffer. Sometimes we do very unhealthy and hurtful things *believing* these behaviors will bring us greater fulfillment or safety or decrease our suffering. We don't know any better. We make *think* we knew better, or we may say, "*No, I knew what I was doing was bad or wrong.*" But in reality, we were still doing the best we could.

> *"If her past were your past, her pain your pain, her level of consciousness your level of consciousness, you would think and act exactly as she does. With this realization comes forgiveness, compassion, peace. The ego doesn't like to hear this, because if it cannot be reactive and righteous anymore, it will lose strength."* –Eckhart Tolle

If you had control over that impulse or knew of another way to get what you were really looking for, you would choose differently. If you knew for certain that choosing differently would actually make you safer in the long term, you would choose it. If you really knew the full consequences of your actions, if you really knew that what you do to another, you do to yourself, if you really knew that we are all connected, your heart would burst open with compassion and your choices would all come out of this unconditional loving.

Begin Noticing when you feel judgment or reactive anger toward someone. For now, there is nothing else to do but notice and track.

At the end of each day, **journal** about these instances. Write down all of the emotions you felt and see if you can identify the underlying beliefs. Take note of all the "shoulds." For example, "He should be more considerate" or "She shouldn't be so angry all the time." Let it all come out with radical honesty.

Afterward, imagine the person you have been judging and say the following to them: "I don't really know what you have gone through that has led you to behave this way. Something painful must have happened that made you believe acting in this manner would bring you greater safety, connection, fulfillment, or relief."

As you do this, observe what releases or holds on within you, allowing either to be okay.

Journaling is an effective medium for expressing emotions and getting to know yourself. Research has shown that people that journal regularly are healthier and happier.

Voice Tone

On the phone, it is the tone of our voice that conveys our acceptance and care for a person. When we are being genuinely empathic, our voice will naturally convey an accepting, caring tone. Coming across like a telephone operator or an interviewer will not build rapport and trust with a caller.

Not everyone is sad and depressed so it is not always effective and appropriate to convey a soft warm voice tone, especially if a person feels frustrated or angry. Instead, **match their voice tone**. This does not mean you should sound frustrated or angry too. It means just be yourself. *When we are being authentic and genuinely empathic with another, our voice will naturally convey a tone that matches theirs.*

There is a lot of information to be gleaned from a person's voice:
- What are they saying?
- What are they *not* saying?
- How do they sound feeling wise?
- Do they speak extremely fast or unusually slow?
- *How* do they speak? Educated? Uneducated?
  Be authentic, but be aware that throwing around big fancy words to an uneducated person can often trigger feelings of inferiority. Feel free to use the words they use – even slang. But do not force it.
- Are they speaking exceptionally loud or soft?
  By keeping our tone a little below or above theirs, they will unconsciously begin to match our tone. We can then keep lowering or raising our tone until they speak at a more desirable level. If they are speaking so softly we cannot understand them, kindly let them know that you are having trouble hearing them. More often than not they will acquiesce and raise their voice.

Silences and Hesitations
Let's say we ask a question and the caller responds with a hesitation or silence. What would this indicate to us? Could this be something difficult to talk about? Has some nerve been struck with this person? Be aware. Do not rush them or force them to respond. *The best response to silence is to let them have it.*

> *"It's okay . . . take your time."*
> *"This sounds like it's something that must be very difficult to talk about."*

For prolonged silences, during or at the onset of a call, assure them that it is okay:

> *"It's okay. When you're ready to talk I'm here to listen."*

If the caller continues to be silent after a minute or two:

> *"It sounds as if you're not quite ready to talk about this yet. That's okay. When you are, we'll be here. We'd like to help. I'm going to end the call now. Please call back any time. Goodnight."*

Silence can allow both you and the caller to adjust to and integrate the information being shared. Often we are so eager trying to "help" that we fail to give the caller the necessary space to share what they need and to take in what we have said.

We convey empathy with our voice tone but we also have to convey it through the words that we speak. How do we do that?

Active listening

> **"When . . . someone really hears you without passing judgment on you, without trying to take responsibility for you, without trying to mold you, it feels darn good. ...When I have been listened to and when I have been heard, I am able to reperceive my world in a new way and to go on. It is astonishing how elements which seem insoluble become soluble when someone listens. How confusions which seemed irremediable turn into relatively clear flowing streams when one is heard."** *–Carl Rogers*

Active listening involves attentive listening, asking open-ended questions, reflecting, and perception checking, and most importantly being empathic and nonjudgmental.

Listening

> **"We have two ears and one mouth, so we should listen more than we say."**
> — *Zeno of Citium*

> **The word 'listen' contains the same letters as the word 'silent'."**
> — *Alfred Brendel*

In order to understand someone better, we have to listen better. Listening is most effective when we really hear what another says. This means evoking curiosity and paying full attention. It also means being fully present with the caller in the moment, leaving all of our beliefs, values, agendas, and interpretations at the door for later.

Listening deeply also invites us to release the need to always think about what we are going to say next.

It is not very helpful to interrupt callers unexpectedly or before they have finished telling their story. Nor can we wait too long to respond or we will come across as dull and passive in the relationship. There is a rhythm to rapport that makes it possible to integrate our response at some natural break or point of conclusion. Callers almost always provide these pauses for us.[1]

Open-Ended Questions

Active listening involves asking questions – **Open-Ended Questions**. While our normal way of questioning produces mostly yes or no or one-word responses, open-ended questions are more like essay questions. They open the door for more self-disclosure and are more like invitations for self-search rather than commands for the production of evidence.[5] Open-ended questions help us to get the Big Picture.

Steer clear of "Why?" questions as best you can because they often come across as judgmental. Why questions also ask for explanations that most persons seeking help are unable to give in a rational or completely logical manner.

There are an endless variety of questions we can ask a caller, but make sure to inquire about the caller's **life situation,** including:

- How their issue is affecting their relationships, work, and/or school life.
- How their issue is affecting eating and sleeping, motivation and focusing.

Examples of Open-Ended Questions:

"What's going on tonight?"
"What would you like to talk about?"
"What happened then?"
"How do you feel about that?"
"When did all this begin?"
"What do you think triggered these feelings?"
"How do you usually cope with this?"
"How has this been affecting your life?"
"Who else have you talked to about this?"

Examples of "Why" questions transformed into Open-Ended Questions:

"Why did you quit your job?"	*"What led you to decide to quit your job?"*
"Why did you hit her?"	*"What led you to decide to hit her?"*
"Why are you sad?"	*"What are you feeling sad about?"*

There *will* be times when we will use a "Why" question. This is okay. But we will develop more trust, a better rapport, and facilitate more self-disclosure and self-awareness with non-why, open-ended questions.

> *"Listening is a magnetic and strange thing, a creative force.*
> *When people really listen to each other in a quiet, fascinated attention,*
> *the creative fountain inside each of us begins to spring and cast up new*
> *thoughts and unexpected wisdom." —Brenda Ueland*

Exploring

Many callers deal only superficially with each topic they bring up. Once a theme or trend is identified, it should be explored in detail. While we should recognize when to delve further, we should also *refrain from probing or prying*. If the caller chooses not to elaborate, we should respect the caller's wishes.

Reflecting and Perception Checking

> *"The message sent is not always the message received." —Virginia Satir*

To let the caller know we are listening and we hear how they are feeling, we reflect back to them. Our role is *to act like mirrors for callers* – reflecting back how they are coming across to us. The key is listening to the **feeling tone of the caller** – hearing between the lines and beneath the words.

> *"You sound sad tonight."*
> *"You seem a little frustrated."*
> *"I'm hearing a lot of pain in your voice."*
> *"You seem down."*
> *"You sound a bit annoyed."*

Often it is in this moment of self-reflection – observing themselves to see if they really *are* feeling this way – that a space of awareness opens up around these emotions. This distancing can diffuse the intensity of their feelings, thus enabling the caller to cope more effectively.

Observing a feeling or thought in ourselves means we are more than those thoughts or feelings, and ultimately we have a *choice* in how to respond. We go from being reactive to responsive.

> *"Looking at something, anything, robs it of its imagined*
> *bigness, toughness, painfulness, and reduces it to a mere*
> *shadow of its former self." —Unknown*

Reflect how they are coming across to you. Do not tell them how they are – *"You are angry"* or *"You are sad."* That comes across as judgmental, and people may become defensive. It also tells them that they are their emotions or personality characteristics. What we really want to do is help them see that they are much more than that, and they have the ability to control and/or change these traits and feelings if they choose.

Repeat a feeling back as often as you hear it.

If, after we reflect a feeling back to them, they disagree and tell us they are not feeling that way, we simply *Buy it back*:

> Listener: *"You sound a little sad tonight."*
> Caller: *"No, I'm not sad."*
> Listener: **"I'm sorry, how are you feeling then?"**

Perception Checking is the skill we use to make sure we are accurately understanding another's communication to us. When they give us a piece of information, we will paraphrase it back to them, asking them if what we heard is accurate. It also helps us to clarify, focus, and let them know we understand. Paraphrase and perception check the most important pieces of information for clarification while focusing on the heart of what they are saying.

> Caller: *"My Dad has been hounding me about cutting the grass, and my mom is always on me about my grades and homework. Meanwhile, my brother and sister won't give me a moment's peace."*
>
> Listener: *"It sounds like you feel frustrated because your family is giving you a hard time."*
>
> Listener: *"It sounds like you're frustrated with your family because you are hoping to have a little personal space and freedom. Is that accurate?"*

Perception Checking is essential because it takes the caller deeper into what they want to say as well as provides feedback about how we are interpreting their message. It can also give them opportunity to explain their idea more thoroughly if they need to.

> *"Do you mean . . ."*
> *"In other words . . ."*
> *"Are you saying . . ."*
> *"What I hear you saying is . . ."*

At first, learning to reflect and perception check may seem awkward. Keep practicing. Start off by practicing the reflection of how the caller sounds (a feeling tone).

> *"You sound frustrated tonight."*

cond, learn to perception check the emotion with the situation.

> *"It sounds like you're feeling frustrated with your family because they are giving you a hard time."*

When you become proficient at this, then you can learn the advanced technique of reflecting back their emotion, situation, and <u>guessing at the underlying hope.</u>

> *"It sounds like you feel frustrated with your family because you are hoping to have a little personal space as well as some peace and quiet."*

Just saying *"You sound frustrated because your family is giving you a hard time"* keeps the focus on the problem and puts responsibility onto the family. By discovering the caller's **deeper hope**, you can focus on what they want. It also allows the caller to see the <u>underlying good intentions beneath the upsetting emotions</u> he or she might feel ashamed about.[2]

Learn and practice each step before moving on to the next one.

Sometimes simply *reflecting back a word or two as part of the next question* can be quite effective. It keeps the flow of the conversation going, focuses on the issue, and opens things up for even more information.

> *"So how do you feel when your <u>Dad yells at you?</u>"*
> *"How do you usually deal with <u>your frustration at work?</u>"*

Keep them focused in the now. How do they feel *now?* If they keep talking about the past, that's okay, but it is more important to know about their feelings now. We cannot change the past, only our interpretation of it, and this is done in the present.

More examples of perception checking:

> *"So you're telling me that your husband won't let you leave the house or even call your friends on the phone, and you are feeling frustrated and trapped because you want him to trust you and you want to have a life of your own. Is this accurate?"*

> *"I hear you. That sounds like that may be very frustrating for you?"*

> *"I'm hearing you say that you feel very lonely and you are not sure how to reach out and connect with others."*

> *"It sounds like your Dad really pushes your buttons."*

> *"Your girlfriend is driving you nuts and you want to scream at her, but at the same time you love her deeply and don't want to risk losing her. Is that right?"*

"And when he criticizes you, how do you feel about that?"

FEELINGS

Most people feel better just talking about their feelings, getting them off their chest. Often, all we want is for someone to listen and empathize. Emotions need to be expressed. The Latin root of emotion means "to move out." Sharing our feelings with another person moves this energy out of ourselves instead of becoming stuck and creating further problems.[1]

Many of us are reluctant to express our feelings. We may have been discouraged or punished for doing so when we were younger, and because of this, have learned to stay in our heads. We use cognitive verbs like I "think" instead of I "feel" which detach us from our feelings.[1] Many callers will focus exclusively on the details of the situation. Focus them back onto their feelings and how they are coping. *After being given a vital piece of information ask open-ended questions like*:

> *"What are you feeling right now?"*

> *"How do you feel about that?"*

Validation

Some callers may be ashamed about what they are feeling. That they should not feel this way. That they are not normal. We want to *validate these feelings*, letting them know it is okay to feel whatever they are feeling.

> *"It's okay to cry."*
> *"It's okay to feel angry or guilty."*
> *"It's alright to feel scared sometimes."*

When feelings are accepted, we are able to explore other elements and feelings that have been suppressed or denied, especially the emotions of guilt, shame, and anger.[3]

The opposite of validation is judgment. *"Don't cry." "Don't feel guilty."* Our intent may be good, but our message is that it is not okay to feel this way. That it is not normal. The caller may end up feeling worse about themselves and more likely to experience this emotion again.

Learning to differentiate emotions and their intensity levels will aid us in sorting out their feelings. There is a big difference between annoyance, anger, and rage. People often feel more than one emotion. Discover all of their feelings.

> *"It sounds like you feel **sad** about your grandmother's death, but also a little **angry** for her being so reckless in her driving. And then **guilty** for feeling angry toward your grandma."*

Normalizing

Normalizing means letting a person know that given their situation and life circumstances, their feelings are normal. Normalizing feelings usually goes hand-in-hand with validating.

> *"It's okay to be angry. I would be angry too if I felt bullied at school."*

> *"It's okay to cry. I cried too when my grandma died."* **Or** . . . *"Most people cry when someone close to them passes away."*

> *"Given what you went through, it is perfectly normal that you would feel helpless."*

Normalizing is most effective after receiving hints of shame behind their feelings.

> *"I can see how you would be feeling angry about this."*

> *"It is not unusual for a person to feel guilt after someone they love dies."*

The best way to help someone is to fully accept them for who they are. Using the listener as a mirror, they can begin to accept themselves. It is in and through empathy, love, and compassion where healing can begin.

Sometimes sharing a personal experience can help normalize a feeling or experience for a caller. Make sure that your intent is to keep the call focused on them even when we are talking about ourselves.

> *"My grandma died a couple of years ago, and I felt real sad for a long time."*

Reinforcement

Some people are very uncomfortable about calling a crisis line and divulging personal information. This may be a new experience for them or they may have bought into the stigma that only crazy people call crisis lines or talk to counselors. Support the caller in feeling more comfortable about their decision to call.

> *"I'm really glad you called tonight."*
> *"It took a lot of courage for you to call."*
> *"You have taken an important first step in calling here tonight."*

This reinforces them to continue seeking support if they need it.

JUDGMENT

"My judgments prevent me from seeing the good that lies behind appearances." –Wayne Dyer.

Example call:

John calls, angry, talking about how he works two jobs he hates in order to pay the bills, then comes home after a couple of drinks to a wife that does nothing but nag him. They argue, and then he hits her in the face a few times. She runs out crying.

After hearing this much of the call, most people are going to have a reaction – a negative one. Such as: *"This guy is a jerk"* or *"I would tell him off"* or *"Someone should take this guy out back and slap <u>him</u> a few times."* When we react this way, we are caught up in judgment, and we don't see clearly. We also lose our centeredness and our empathy. The call becomes about us instead of them.

We know how we feel, but we do not know how he feels. He obviously called the line for a reason, most likely not to brag. Could he be sorry about his actions? Could he feel guilty, knowing he was wrong, but not knowing what else to do? *Letting go of judgments does not alleviate people's responsibility for their actions!*

"No man consciously chooses evil because it is evil; he only mistakes it for the happiness he seeks." –Mary Wollstonecraft Shelly

Becoming judgmental makes situations worse. How do you think he would react if we became angry or judgmental toward him? He would probably get defensive, more angry and even hang up. It is easy to feel for the woman who was assaulted. We obviously want to help *her*. But she is not the one on the phone right now. So what is the best way to help her? Help him.

Contrary to what some people believe, everyone is doing their best in life to cope. Everyone is trying to find love and safety and freedom. Some people just go about it in very unhealthy ways. But if they knew a better way, and trusted in that choice, they would no doubt use it.

Under this man's anger, violence, and defensiveness is hiding unresolved fear, shame, and hurt. He feels fragile and scared of being hurt even more. So big walls go up, and he lashes out before he can be hurt again. People who seem to be spewing hate are projecting their feelings of being unloved. They feel hated.

"The hatred you see directed outward is actually pain being exposed by a person who is experiencing it." –Wayne Dyer

We are not encouraging you to accept this man's actions as being okay, but rather to accept his actions as having already occurred. Becoming angry and judgmental does not change things and certainly does not change people for the better. If we really want to help the world and the victims of anger and violence, we must understand why they do what they do. Anger and hatred are best diffused with empathy and compassion, not more anger and hatred.

> ***"Will that be the goal of your life as a psychologist and as a human being; changing others to make life more comfortable for yourself?"*** *–Power of Empathy*

Identify with the hurt. Think that it must be hard to carry around all that anger, that hurt, that fear. Know that feeling in yourself.

Feeling for him does not mean we do not feel for the victim.

Get his story. Find out how he feels, perception check, and be empathic with him. When we get to problem solving, we can generate ways he can respond differently – healthier – next time.

We all have values. We are not asking you to give them up. We are encouraging you to understand *the caller's* view of the world and not impose yours on them. That is why we say **the reality of the caller is the reality of the call.**

When we become judgmental, what we are doing is creating a boundary, a wall between us and them. "I am good, and you are bad." We are setting up a conflict between us and them. Each time we do this our body will alert us by causing a physical reaction and creating an uncomfortable emotion such as anger, annoyance, or some form of irritation. The stronger the judgment, the more intense the emotional reaction and physical tension. So every time they say or do the very thing that bothers us, we react with anger. It's as if they are pushing our buttons. They say or do something – we react. **We have given our power away.** And our reactive anger does not change the situation or him for the better. It only changes us, causing us to feel terrible.

> ***"The strain of constant judgment is virtually intolerable. It is curious that an ability so debilitating would be so deeply cherished."*** *–A Course in Miracles.*

Noticing our upset feelings is our signal that we have made a negative judgment. Do not suppress the feelings, just be aware of them. This allows us to choose how to respond in a more neutral, curious manner.

People do not like talking to others who are judgmental. Think of the people in your life that are like this. Do you like to talk to them? Is this the person you would open up to and be vulnerable with?

> *"Judging keeps us on the outside of relationships when*
> *we really belong on the inside." – On Becoming a Counselor*

Judgment is at the root of most of our social problems. Biases based on titles, ethnic heritage, race, religion, and physical appearances invariably cause confusion and hostility, making it difficult for us to relate to each other.[4] Overt prejudices are not the only obstacles to empathic listening. We all have developed ways of organizing our world by putting people in categories and attaching labels to certain behaviors. We often assume that our beliefs about people and things are the objective truth because our beliefs are commonly held by our social group, and our peers regularly validate our perceptions.[2]

What disturbs you? Abortion? Homosexuality? A different race? Violent people? Selfishness?

A negative reactive judgment cuts right to the core of a person. It says that person is bad. It fails to make a discernment between a person's essence and their personality or behavior. It puts us in a position of superiority and our goal becomes to withdraw from, attack, or change others. If we can find common ground with this person, we are then able to empathize and our goal now becomes to connect with and support them.

People do hurtful things because their view of themselves is negative. When we accept them just as they are and reflect back to them that we see them as good, whole, and perfect at their core, their view of themselves can begin to shift toward the positive and, with that, their behaviors and thoughts and emotions become more life-enhancing.

> *Judgments are mental and emotional violence.*

Quick Review:

We have opened the call with a professional and warm greeting. We have gotten their name and age and are letting them take the lead with an opener such as, *"What can I help you with tonight?"* or *"What's going on tonight?"* We have developed rapport and gained their trust by being empathic and nonjudgmental, matching their voice tone while perception checking and reflecting back information and feelings. Each one of the caller's specific feelings have been validated and normalized as we gather the Big Picture. Now is a great time to **summarize** before moving on.

Summarization

Summarizing helps you to organize your thoughts and information. It also works to feed back this information to the caller for *clarification* – making sure our *perception* of their needs and feelings is the same as theirs. This also allows us to focus on the core issue that we are going to be working on.

> *"So, let me make sure I've got all this . . . Your grandma died two weeks ago and you're feeling sad, a little angry, and guilty about feeling angry. You feel like you have no one to talk to about this, and you can't seem to concentrate or get any work done. Is this correct?"*

There can be a lot of information over the course of the call to remember, so it always helps to write down vital pieces as you go along. If you are ever at a loss for words during a call and do not know what to ask next, go into a summary. It will help you recollect your thoughts.

Summarizing is always recommended before moving into any kind of problem solving.

PROBLEM SOLVING

"Counseling is not a task to be accomplished but a relationship to be experienced. We are not solving a puzzle, but trying to respond to a person." – On Becoming a Counselor

Problem solving only begins after everything we have discussed thus far is taken care of. *You must get the entire Big Picture and deal with their feelings first.* A person will not be able to think rationally if they do not deal with their emotions first.

Now, our goal as crisis workers is not to solve their problems. It is to get them through the night. Most callers will have deeper, more entrenched issues and trauma that will require long-term care and therapy to resolve. We are not providing long-term help. We are here for crisis intervention, immediate emotional support, and referrals to agencies and therapists that *can* provide long-term help.

Most people's first instinct is to jump right in and try to fix the problem. There is a tendency to avoid feelings by jumping into problem solving and advice giving instead of listening. Without some degree of connection at the feeling level, the emotional imbalance will not be restored and their upset feelings will remain stuck, eventually becoming toxic. *Become aware of your need to fix, rescue, or have the caller change.* Just notice these urges, which often manifest as impatience, eagerness, and tension. Rather than judging yourself or trying to force these urges away, empathize with the part of yourself that wants to fix, rescue, or caretake this person. Then ask that part to step back, knowing that the best way to help someone change is by not trying to change them at all. It is to accept them just as they are.

This is our foundation – acceptance. When we experience the desire to fix and feel tension to some degree, we have lost our foundation and the call begins to become about us and our agenda for them. Take a breath, empathize with the part of yourself that wants to solve it for them, and then go back to listening and using your skills like perception checking and reflecting.

It is our belief that people have the answers inside of themselves. We are here to support them to find those solutions in mutual discovery. **We do not give advice**. To give advice is to keep callers in a state of dependence upon the judgment and guidance of others. It can be a reinforcer of helplessness rather than empowerment.

When you feel the urge to give advice and want to say:

> *"You need to dump that guy."*
> *"You should see a doctor."*
> *"You should tell her how you feel."*

Notice the urge, ask inwardly for that part of you to step back, and then instead **offer a suggestion or a question.**

> *"What would it be like if you weren't in this relationship?"*
> *"Have you thought about going to a doctor?"*
> *"What would happen if you told her how you feel?"*

"You should . . ." can be turned into *"Have you considered . . .?"*

People will often ask for your advice. And when they do, you **turn it back on them.**

> Caller: *"What do you think I should do about this?"*
> Listener: *"What do **you** think you could do?"*

Sometimes callers feel helpless and want someone else to provide all the answers. They may persist in wanting you to tell them what to do. Keep the focus on them.

> Listener: *"Everybody's different, so let's find out what's right for **you**."*

> Or   *"This call is not about what **I** think, it's about what **you** think."*

> Or   *"It sounds as if you are confused and a bit frustrated over what to do and are hoping to get some answers. Let's see if we can't figure something out together."*

Focus the caller toward self-responsibility. It is never helpful to a caller to agree in seeing them as helpless, powerless, or victims in any situation. Help them to realize they are the ones that can make changes and new choices.

A good starting point is to find out what their **goals** are.

> *"What would you like to see happen?"*

"What would be your ideal outcome?"
"How would you like to feel?"
"Where would you like to be in one year? Three years?"

When they provide us with some of this information, it will help us focus the call in a more specific direction. Work together on coming up with one or two *small steps* toward this goal or ideal outcome.

Gathering more information will be the key. Get to know what *they* would like to try, what *they* have tried before, how *they* usually go about solving their problems, and how *they* have felt about the outcomes and results. Get them actively involved in the problem solving process.

"What have you thought of trying?"
"How did that work out for you?"
"How did you feel about that?"
"What else have you tried to do?"
"How did that work?"
"How have you been dealing with this?"
"How do you usually solve problems?"
"How do you usually deal with stress?"
"Have you been in a similar situation before?"
"Who else can you talk to?"
"Have you talked to anyone else about this?"
"Do you have any hobbies or interests?"

Use open-ended questions. If they are comfortable with an idea, then look at all the possible outcomes, consequences, and feelings with each choice.

Throughout the problem solving portion, we will continue gathering information, reflecting, perception checking, summarizing, validating, normalizing, as well as being empathic, accepting, and nonjudgmental.

Resource Ring
Callers may experience stress because they believe they do not have any choices, support, or alternatives. Assist them in seeing the choices and support they have by using what is called a Resource Ring.

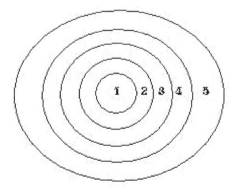

1. Self
2. Friends, Neighbors, Relatives
3. Persons Helpful in the Past
4. Community Resources
5. Emergency Resources

It starts at the center with the caller's own self, then moves out to family, friends, and neighbors. The third ring is exploring persons that have been helpful in the past to the caller. Community and Emergency resources occupy the fourth and fifth rings. These include schools, churches, counselors, clinics, helplines, etc.

Often, callers do not think of these kinds of resources when a problem or crisis occurs. Begin by discussing resources from the inside rings outward, discovering what the caller has at their disposal to aid in reaching goals.

What if I have suggestions for the caller?
Always generate alternatives with the caller first. After we have exhausted those, we can bring up other resources or ideas we may have.

> *"Have you tried journaling?"*
> *"Have you ever considered seeing a counselor?"*
> *"Would you consider an anger management course?"*
> *"How does that sound to you?"*
> *"Is this something that you might be willing to try?"*
> *"One suggestion for your consideration that works well for dissipating anger is journal writing."*

When discussing options, assist callers in talking each one through to its likely conclusion. In other words, help them anticipate what is likely to happen if they pursue each alternative and how they are likely to feel about each possible outcome. When they respond with any kind of emotion, label it and reflect it back.

Educating
We do not give advice as listeners, but we can provide information. Make sure you know what you are talking about though. *Do not give information you are not qualified to give.* You are not a physician, nurse or pharmacist (unless you are of course). However, we can use the references at our disposal or the Internet to share information, prefacing with, *"According to the reference I have here . . ."*

Focusing
Focusing on a single idea or area of concern can help us and the caller to zone in on the heart of a problem. This is especially useful when the caller jumps rapidly from one thought to another.

> *"This point seems worth looking at more closely."*
> *"You've mentioned several things. Let's talk a bit about . . ."*
> *"Tell me more about . . ."*

Sometimes a caller will focus exclusively on the details of their situation instead of their feelings. Focus them back onto their feelings. This will help the caller express themselves and think more clearly.

> *"You have told me a lot about the situation. I would like to hear how this has affected you and what your feelings are."*

What <u>not</u> to say:

<u>Playing expert or know-it-all</u>. When you don't know something, don't pretend that you do.

> Caller*:*   *"I've got this rash on my groin area."*
> Listener: *"My Dad usually says to just mix up some oil and butter and*
> *spread it on the area. Should be good as new."*

Be honest and tell them you do not know. Give them a referral to someone who does. It is okay not to know. Be aware of trying to play expert. Even professional therapists must know their limitations.

<u>Reassurance</u>: Attempting to dispel the caller's anxiety by implying there is no reason for it to exist is to completely devalue the caller's own feelings and experience.

> *"I wouldn't worry about it."*
> *"Everything will be alright."*
> *"Turning forty isn't so bad. You're still young."*

<u>Defending</u>: To defend what the caller has criticized is to imply that they have no right to express their impressions, opinions, or feelings.

> *"I'm sure she didn't mean it that way."*
> *"I'm sure that he has your welfare in mind when he . . ."*
> *"Yeah, but, you know your mother loves you."*

<u>Belittling feelings</u>: Sometimes in an attempt to normalize, we minimize and belittle the caller's intense and overwhelming feelings with the undertone, "It's no big deal."

> *"Everyone gets down in the dumps."*
> *"Buck up."*
> *"It's just a phase everyone goes through."*

<u>Interpreting</u>: To interpret is to seek to make conscious that which is unconscious, telling the caller the meaning of his or her experiences. Only a professional counselor is prepared to do this, and even then, a person should discover their own meanings considering we all see the world slightly differently. Interpreting is not our role.

"What you really mean is . . ."
"Unconsciously you're saying . . ."
"This is because of what happened to you when you were a child."

Resources and Referrals

When the extent of the help they need is beyond us, the best way for us to help is to offer referrals to places that can provide the caller with some longer term or more specific help.

Know your limitations and the limitations of the services you provide and offer them a referral. However, we also do not want to be too quick in throwing referrals at them. Listen and get the Big Picture first before making any decisions, unless it is an emergency, which will be discussed in later sections.

The referral should be gentle and constructive rather than a reaction made out of our own anxiety and helplessness.

Make sure to get all of their information. What city do they live in? Do they have insurance? Do not discuss any fees. Explain what we are doing when looking up a resource. We have many referral resources to choose from. Getting to know some of the resources available can increase your self-confidence, reduce stress, and make the process of referral much easier on both caller and listener.[1]

If they do not like a referral, explore other ones. When you have agreed on something, make a plan to implement it, then walk them through it. Prepare them for what to expect if you can. When giving a referral, ask the caller to write it down and repeat it back to you in order to make sure the information has been written down correctly.

Wrapping up a call

When you feel that the call has gone about as far as it is going to go, the best way to wrap up is to ask what the caller is going to do later that day or tomorrow. Talk about implementing the options that have been discussed. Encourage **small steps**, and *make a plan.* Create a road map of what the caller can do and walk them through it. After all, a good idea is only that until we implement it.

Your voice can have a quality of finality to it . . .

> *"I think we've gone as far as we can in this call. I'm going to keep the lines open for other callers now."*

> *"Well, I hope this works out for you. I won't take up anymore of your time."*
> *"I'm glad you called. I hope it's helped you. Call back anytime if you need to."*

"We've discussed a lot. Why don't you take some time to think about it, then if you need to, feel free to call us back."

Patience

***"Empathy's most enduring characteristic is that quality
of focused, patient attentiveness." –Power of Empathy***

Being patient is an important quality when listening to people. Be aware of trying to rush someone off the phone or forcing someone to open up too soon. Notice any part you that feels frustrated when talking to the callers you consider resistant or difficult. This is an indication that you are expecting them to be something they are not. It is a judgment.
At the same time, remember patience is not the same thing as doing nothing. Pace yourself to meet the caller's way of communicating but keep the conversation moving in a suitable direction using active listening skills.[5]

Authenticity

***"Each person has a sacred uniqueness, which requires
of us a reaction which cannot be prepared beforehand.
It demands nothing of what is past. It demands presence,
responsibility. It demands us." –Martin Buber***

Be aware of retreating into analyzing and diagnosing, seeing this human as a case, psychological burden, or annoying time-occupier. When you are being authentic, it should feel more like being in love than solving a mystery.

Also, be aware of trying to give a good response rather than responding to the person. Becoming self-conscious in an effort to sound like an accomplished therapist will make us less aware of the person we are trying to help. Listening with true empathy, we help others think in terms of what they want for themselves rather than what they should do.[2]

Self-Awareness
Therapeutic awareness means being conscious of our own emotions, values, opinions, and behavior. Understanding our own psychological processes and dynamics can help guide another through his or her processes. If we have not worked through our own issues, our own feelings may interfere with the ability to remain calm, curious, compassionate, and caller focused.[6]

EMPATHY DEVELOPMENT

Releasing Judgments
Exercise #1

<u>Judgments are the biggest barrier to Empathy.</u>

<u>The first step is to become aware of what our judgments are.</u>

For **one week** observe your own judgments about other people. Whenever you are upset or triggered by another person's behavior, notice it, then write down the quality in them that is most upsetting to you.

Look at your list at the end of the week. What qualities came up the most? Are there a few that keep coming up? Write down the five qualities that upset you the most.

1._____

2._____

3._____

4._____

5._____

These are the ones you will be working with throughout the training and hopefully after.

EXERCISES IN THE PERCEPTION OF FEELINGS*

Read each message and write the feelings involved in the space provided. As you complete each exercise, check the feelings you identified with those given by the authors. If you were unsuccessful in identifying the feelings correctly, study the message further to see whether you can discover the cues you missed.

Remember, while it is effective and necessary to learn how to identify feelings, we never want to assume or jump to any conclusions about a caller's feeling states. Always ask.

1. "Life just doesn't seem worth struggling with anymore. I just don't think I can make it. I just can't go on anymore."
Feelings Involved:_____

2. "I think this is just a complete waste of time! I never wanted to come. I wouldn't be here if my husband didn't make me. I don't know why I should be here! He has more problems than me!"
Feelings Involved:_____

3. "I don't shower after gym. I'm embarrassed about my body, about being overweight."
Feelings Involved:_____

4. "I wonder if I do too much for my husband. He doesn't do much for me or for any woman. I knocked myself out painting the house, and he didn't lift a finger to help me."
Feelings Involved:_____

5. (Fourteen year old boy:) "I don't feel I'm ever considered at all. Everybody tells me to do this, do that. All I am is a thing."
Feelings Involved:_____

6. (Woman:) "The house is just constantly in turmoil. I never seem to have any peace or a minute for myself. I just sit down and the kids are either fighting, or they want me to wait on them, or something happens. I can't ever sit down to rest and enjoy a TV show or read a magazine."
Feelings Involved:_____

7. "I know my children are busy, but wouldn't you think they could find time to at least call their mother on the telephone to see if she is dead or alive?"
Feelings Involved:_____

8. (Girl:) "I'm going to leave home. No matter what I do I'm always wrong. My mother keeps telling me my dresses are too short, that I'm going to get in trouble with boys. I can't stand it any longer. I'm going to run away."
*Feelings Involved:*_____

9. "I decided to go to the dance after the football game, but it was a real drag. I didn't dance a single dance. I've had it with the boys in our school. They're a bunch of creeps."
*Feelings Invovled:*_____

10. "I can't tolerate my husband's flirting. Last night at a party you can't believe how attentive he was to that divorced floozie from work. I'd swear he talked more to her last night than to me. When I told him that afterwards, he got uptight and told me it was all in my head."
Feelings Involved:_____

* Exercises used from the book, *Improving Therapeutic Communication*. (pp. 90-96).[7]

Answers To Feelings Identification Exercises:

1. Depressed, despondent, in despair, demoralized, overwhelmed, helpless, defeated, hopeless, worthless.

2. Angry, resentful, bitter, indignant, antagonistic, controlled, dominated, unjustly coerced, put upon, unfairly blamed.

3. Embarrassed, ashamed, self-conscious, humiliated, horrible, afraid of ridicule or criticism, inadequate, inferior, deficient, exposed.

4. Confused, perplexed, frustrated, disconcerted, irritated, resentful, used, aggravated.

5. Hurt, overlooked, depreciated, devalued, ignored, unappreciated, rejected, dominated, bossed, controlled, resentment, anger.

6. Burdened, pressured, overwhelmed, exhausted, frustration, in turmoil, unfulfilled, deprived, powerless, immobilized, aggravated, annoyed, irritated, agitated.

7. Neglected, unappreciated, lonesome, hurt, let down, indignant, bitter, resentful, angry.

8. Angry, offended, put upon, resentful, antagonistic, unjustly accused, unfairly criticized, fed up, never understood, picked on, hurt, degraded, belittled, hopeless, alienated, rejected.

9. Disappointed, disgusted, fed up, mad, ticked off, left out, rejected, hurt, lonely, inadequate, lacking, unimportant.

10. Jealous, angry, aggravated, indignant, irked, chagrined, insecure, hurt, afraid (fear of rejection and abandonment).

TOOLS AND RESOURCES FOR ANXIOUS CALLERS

*"This is the most important question a human being
needs to answer: Is the universe a friendly place or not?"*
—Albert Einstein

Anxiety may be the most common struggle for people calling a crisis line. From simple concerns to chronic worry to full blown panic, anxiety often underlies or runs alongside all of the other reported issues.

Helping callers "regulate" or cope with their anxiety so they can think rationally and make informed decisions requires us to have some tools at our disposal.

Breathe: It seems fairly obvious that taking a few deep breaths can help us slow down, calm ourselves, and regulate. Yet, so often we don't do it. We may have to remind the caller to do this.

> *"It sounds like this situation is causing you a lot of anxiety. Let's start by getting some more oxygen into your system with a couple of breaths. That way you'll be able to think more clearly."*

> *"I really hear how frightened you are right now. I'm here for you. You are not alone. Since there is no immediate danger, shall we try a short breathing exercise to help the part of you that feels so scared?"*

Breathe with the person. Do it together.

A five count breathing exercise can be effective for some. Counting to five on the inhale, hold for a five count, then exhale slowly for five. Repeat until they feel more settled.

If the caller resists the breathing exercise or it makes them feel worse, then don't do it.

Ask them to rate their anxiety on a scale of 1-10. 10 being panic and 1 being like still water on a lake, absolute calm. If their rating is 8 or higher, here are two techniques you can utilize to help them feel a little calmer:

Finding Colors: Ask them to locate something in their space that is red. After they do this, then choose another color (blue, purple, black, etc.). Do this for at least seven different colors, then have them report if their level of anxiety has shifted. What this does is help to *distract* their internal worrying mind and focus on something external.

Tossing an object from hand to hand, such as a full water bottle, a ball, sandbag, or any other object that has a little weight to it, can often help a person reduce high anxiety levels. It serves as a partial distraction while bringing the person more into their body. It also helps the two hemispheres of the brain to connect and communicate with one other, which can be helpful for soothing upset feelings.

If their rating is 7 or lower, then start with some breathing then try one or more of the following if you sense it would be helpful to the caller during the call.

Self-talk: Ask the caller to locate the anxiety in their body. If they can do this, then have them place their hand on that part of their body. Often it is the chest, heart, or abdomen. Then ask them "What does the afraid part need to hear from you right now?" If an answer comes to them then have them repeat these phrases to the anxious part.

> *"Everything is going to be okay."*
> *"I'm here for you."*
> *"You are not alone."*
> *"You are safe now."*
> *"You are not going to get in trouble."*

You can repeat these phrases to the caller for additional reinforcement.

Grounding: Guide the caller to focus their awareness into their body, as best as they can, beginning with their feet. Have them feel their feet on the ground, feel gravity, then their ankles, noticing and allowing whatever sensations they can, followed by their shins, calves, knees, upper legs, hips, back, abdomen, chest, shoulders, arms, neck, face, head. Guide them throughout to feel the energy of gravity pulling downwards, connecting them to the Earth. Take it slow to help their system to slow down.

LONELINESS

You would be hard pressed to find anyone who has not experienced feelings of loneliness at some point in their life. It seems to be a part of the human condition.

Loneliness is a sad feeling resulting from a perceived separation of some form, such as the new college student away from home for the first time, or being separated from a loved one due to death or divorce. Even the person with a large amount of friends can still feel lonely if cut off from oneself or one's larger purpose. Pulling away or isolating oneself to protect from being hurt again can often engender an experience of loneliness as well.

People naturally desire connection – to themselves, others, nature, a higher power. Some people feel the need for connection more than others.

> *"You're always alone, but you're only lonely if you*
> *don't like the person you're alone with." –Wayne Dyer*

When we are not comfortable with ourselves, a certain degree of loneliness is bound to emerge. The more we dislike ourselves, the greater the degree of loneliness.

Many lonely people lack confidence in themselves, and/or lack adequate "people skills," unfamiliar to appropriate boundaries and etiquette. They may feel awkward, talk too much or too little, reveal too much too soon, or speak offensively.

It is important to differentiate callers who have not developed adequate social skills from those who know how to meet and interact with others but have chosen not to or are prevented from it. When a lonely person chooses to turn to a telephone crisis hotline for assistance, it usually means that they have lost, to some degree, confidence in their ability to encounter and become close to others.[5]

Taking the loneliness call:

In order to determine the most effective way to assist a lonely caller, you have to assess what they need. In order to do that, the <u>Big Picture</u> must be gathered first. Get their name and age, then ask *open-ended questions* to find out the **reasons for their call.**

> *"What is your name?"*
> *"How old are you?"*
> *"What's going on tonight?"*
> *"Did something happen?"*
> *"What do you think triggered these feelings?"*
> *"How long have you been feeling this way?"*
> *"How do you feel about that?"*

Make sure the caller is okay. If there is any indication they or another might be in danger, do not hesitate to **check their safety.**

> *"Are you okay?"*
> *"Where are you?"*
> *"Is anyone else there?"*
> *"Do you feel safe?"*

Ask about their current life situation. Sleeping? Eating? Depression? etc.

> *"Did something recently change in your life?"*
> *"How are you feeling about that?"*
> *"How have you been dealing with this?"*
> *"How has your life been affected?"*

Do not try to fix them or solve their problems. Just listen and empathize. In many instances, simply expressing interest and care while allowing the callers to talk will be enough.

Reflect back their feelings and do Perception Checking. Make sure you clearly understand what they are saying, the meanings of what they are sharing, and how they are feeling.

> *"You sound down tonight."*
> *"You seem kind of lonely."*
> *"It sounds like you are really down on yourself right now. Is that right?"*
> *"So what I hear you saying is that you feel sad because you believe nobody in school likes you. Is this accurate?"*
> *"I really hear how important being in a relationship is to you. Can you tell me more about this?"*

Be warm, empathic and nonjudgmental. This will build the trust and rapport that is needed to facilitate any emotional healing. Remember, they don't need to be fixed or rescued. They need to know they are capable, good at their core, and are being supported.

Validate and Normalize their feelings.

> *"It's okay to feel lonely. It makes sense that you would feel this way, under the circumstances. I would be surprised if you didn't feel this way."*

If they are crying, let them cry.

> *"It's okay to cry. Take your time."*
> *"It's okay to let that emotion come up. You don't have to hold it in with me."*

Sometimes sharing a personal experience can help normalize a caller's feelings and empower them with hope.

> *"When I moved out of my house, I felt lonely for a long time. Then I realized it was up to me to do something about it, so I took some classes and read some books to learn about myself, and eventually little by little I built some strong friendships and developed better feelings about myself."*

Always keep the focus of the call about the caller. If you do share a personal experience, share it authentically with the intention to normalize and validate their feelings and experience. Never let the call become about you.

Investigate the caller's *past history of social relationships*, attempts at relationships, and the feelings involved with both.

Explore whether the caller is defining their self-worth by the positive or negative outcomes of their encounters. When an attempt fails, for whatever reason, they may be interpreting the failure as a sign of personal inadequacy – that they are a loser, stupid, ugly, bad, etc. In this context, the idea of approaching others becomes much more threatening and fear producing. This sets up a self-fulfilling prophecy as they become even more anxious and/or withdrawn.

Only out of acceptance for oneself and one's feelings can one grow and make new choices. Bottled up or unacknowledged feelings indicate shame which can lead to disconnection, alienation, and separation.

What are some of their **hobbies and interests? Expectations? Dreams?**

> *"How would you like to feel?"*
> *"What would you like to see happen?"*
> *"What do you like to do?"*
> *"What would be your ideal outcome?"*

Explore the caller's Resource Ring.

> *"What have you thought about doing?"*
> *"What have you tried?"*
> *"Have you talked with anyone else about your feelings?"*
> *"How did they respond?"*
> *"How about co-workers? People at church? A therapist?"*

Be creative in helping the caller come up with more options than they previously thought they had. Allow the caller to generate ideas first, and then we can offer suggestions of our own. <u>Do not give advice</u>. People who feel lonely often yearn to be more assertive and feel more empowered, even though they may feel more comfortable and safe playing a victim role. By giving them answers and advice, we disempower them even more.

40

<u>Always encourage small steps.</u> Reinforce the fact they reached out for help.

> *"I'm glad you called. This is a great first step."*

Lonely callers may indulge in a great deal of paralyzing self-pity and helplessness. Make sure their feelings of helplessness are gently reflected and validated.

> *"It sounds like you feel really helpless about your situation. Is that right?"*
> *"Feeling pretty helpless right now, huh?"*

If, through the process of problem solving, they continue to feel helpless, we may wish to gently <u>confront</u>:

> *"I really hear how hard this is for you and how hopeless this seems to be. I'm wondering what it would take for you to see this situation differently."*

> *"What part do you think you play in this interaction with your husband?"*

> *"If you were to reach out to others more, what is your concern would happen?"*

> *"I'm wondering what the part of you that feels helpless needs?"*

> *"If you were the wisest, most compassionate person in the world, what advice would you give yourself regarding this situation?"*

This last example can be a wonderful and effective way to facilitate the realization of a person's own inner wisdom.

If the caller seems unwilling to take any action, a gentle reminder that they will continue to be lonely and sad until they choose to do something about their situation or choose to view their situation differently may be in order. Always be aware of your own need to fix, change, or rescue the caller. The best indication of this is when you begin experiencing frustration with this person.

Working with lonely callers often takes a lot of patience, time, and empathy on your part. At the same time, it is not our function to provide "telephone friendships." When a caller is no longer willing to do the work, it is time to end the call and the telephone relationship.

Empathy and Loneliness

> ***"Those who are awake have one world in common.***
> ***Those who are asleep live each in a separate world."*** *– Heraclites*

Journal on a time in your life when you felt lonely. What were your feelings? What did you feel was missing from your life? From yourself? How did you feel about yourself? If you eventually worked through it, what sort of steps did you take? What would you have wanted from people when you were feeling lonely?

Notice any judgments, frustration or discomfort you have when discussing loneliness with a caller. Just notice (do not judge yourself – it is normal), and then reinvest yourself in being curious with the intention to understand their unique view of the world.

Empathize with all the caller's feelings. Know that they are trying the best they can to cope and find happiness, love and acceptance.

> ***"How can I have empathy for others without having***
> ***empathy for myself?"*** *– Gandhi*

Empathy Exercise: Choose a person you feel strong judgment toward. Pretend you are this person. Why are they acting this way? What happened in their past to cause them to act this way? What are they really searching for deep down? Create a life history (even if it is made up by you) that would explain why they do as they do. See the world through their eyes. Do this until you feel the judgment dissolving and compassion coming forward.

DEPRESSION

Statistics:

- Depression affects more than 16.1 million American adults, or about 6.7% of the U.S. population age 18 and older in a given year, according to the National Institute of Mental Health.[8]
- In 2015, the World Health Organization estimated 322 million people were living with depression, making it the leading cause of ill health and disability worldwide.[9]
- Women are almost 2 times more likely than men to become depressed.[8]
- 67% of people with depression do not actively seek nor receive proper treatment. [8]
- 54% of people believe depression is a personal weakness.[10]

The major differences between loneliness and depression are:

- *The degree to which one's life is affected.* A greater degree of imbalance and energy loss is associated with depression. This imbalance can occur to the point that the person might not be able to function.
- *More shame.* The person who is depressed experiences more shame and self-anger than a person who is just lonely.
- *More disconnection.* With depression there are often stronger feelings of aloneness, disconnection, and alienation.

As with loneliness, most people have experienced the feeling of being down in the dumps from time to time. However, the duration and intensity of these feelings vary widely from person to person. Certain people seem to be more prone to depression than others.

Symptoms and complaints of depression:

- Feeling sad, lonely, down.
- Feeling tired, lacking energy, exhausted.
- Feeling excessively self critical, worthless, shameful.
- Feeling empty, hollow, lifeless, dead.
- Changes in sleep patterns – insomnia, wanting to sleep too much or not at all.
- Changes in eating patterns – eating too much or not at all.
- Disinterest in everything and anyone.
- Irritability.
- Feelings of dread.
- Concentration problems.
- Withdrawal or isolating behavior.
- Vague complaints about bodily symptoms, backaches, headaches.
- Exaggerated excitement – person looks as if they are trying too hard to appear happy.
- Thinking is negative and pessimistic, narrow and rigid.

Why Depression?

There is no one definitive answer as to why people get depressed. The uninformed majority generally believe it is caused by some triggering event of loss or separation such as:

- Death of a loved one.
- A separation or divorce.
- Loss of a job or retirement.
- Illness or accident (loss of abilities, skills).
- A humiliating event (loss of self-esteem or self-worth).

It is true enough that a major loss or separation can have a significant impact on *triggering* a depression, but the loss itself is not the cause. Two people can suffer the same loss yet experience it two different ways. It is how we *perceive* a loss that affects how we *react* to a loss.

Some argue that depression is caused by biological factors such as an imbalance of chemicals and neurotransmitters in the brain. This is true, but more than likely only partially true. Chemicals are released in our body after thinking certain thoughts or memories. Most prolonged imbalances are the result of thought and belief patterns which perpetuate the release of these chemicals. In return, these chemicals influence our thinking, thus engendering the release of even more chemicals creating a cycle.

Blaming the body or genetic predispositions can allow people to deflect responsibility for their own feeling and mental states. The perceived painful work of looking within themselves is avoided for the much simpler solutions of taking pills or doing nothing. Exceptions may include some mental disorders such as schizophrenia and bipolar disorder, as well as some head traumas.

Depression is often the result of negative beliefs about ourselves. Beliefs that foster a sense of lack and shame about who we are. These beliefs are heavily influenced by *other* beliefs called expectations.

EXPECTATIONS

"A man cannot be comfortable without his own approval." –Mark Twain

Expectations are the beliefs we have about ourselves and the world. It is our particular view of reality with the demand that everything fit to conform to this view. Expectations are the way we think we "*should*" be, the way we believe other people "*should*" be, or the way the world "*should*" be.

When expectations are turned upon the self, we create goals and make demands that place pressure upon ourselves to live up to these goals. These goals are often based upon <u>ideals</u> and values we have internalized from our culture and family of origin. The difference between how we perceive ourselves now and how we think we should be (our ideal) leaves a gap. This gap creates a feeling of being flawed, inferior, less than, not enough. The greater the gap, the stronger the negative feelings of disappointment, anger, and shame we will have toward ourselves for not measuring up.

> ***"Peace is the result of retraining your mind to process
> life as it is, rather than as you think it should be."*** *–Wayne Dyer*

When internalized, the expectations to be "superwoman" – perfect looks, perfect family and relationship, have a career, and to be kind and giving all the time – can create enormous stress and pressure for women. Men often expect themselves to be "super achievers," striving endlessly to acquire lots of money, power and high status, material goods, while never showing a hint of weakness. Men also feel pressure to have the perfect looks and physique now more than ever.

The media and advertisers influence our expectations. In trying to sell their products to us through the mediums of television, radio, magazines, and the internet, corporations are conditioning us to think in a certain way. They would like us to believe that we need their products in order to feel better about ourselves and avoid rejection.

We internalize these messages and ideals, and then we strive endlessly to live up to them. Why is it so important to be perfect and to live up to these ideals?

**All striving to live up to expectations is really a desire for
acceptance and safety.**

Our parents had an enormous influence on our approval seeking patterns. When we were young, parents approved of some things we did and disapproved of other things. It was very important to get our parents' approval. In fact, we felt our very survival as a human depended upon it. The aspects of our personality that were disapproved of got shoved down and repressed. The more non-accepting, unresponsive, critical, or misattuned our parents were, the more we had to repress, and the harder we had to work to win their approval. As we got older, we internalized our parents' voices and eventually heard them as our own. We took these voices with us out into the world and then generalized our beliefs about approval to society.

From the moment we are born we are ranked and measured. Parents compare and brag about their kids to other parents. Schools perpetuate the addiction to comparison and ranking with gold stars, grades, degrees, awards, SATs, GREs, GPAs, etc. We are told how to feel about ourselves and are treated differently based upon where we are ranked. We thus equate our identity and value as a human being with our roles, looks, grades, jobs, accomplishments and possessions. What each culture values may be slightly different, but the pressures and beliefs to conform are still there – and they can be incredibly powerful determinants of our thoughts, feelings, and behaviors.

These internalized expectations of how we *should* be and what we *should* do in order to feel worthy create suffering for ourselves. We worry we will not be able to keep up with everyone else. We strive harder and harder but never seem to get closer to the acceptance and safety, happiness and peace that we seek. So we try harder and do more, believing a better job, more schooling, more money, or a bigger house will get us there.

> *"When we are angry or depressed in our creativity, we have misplaced our power. We have allowed someone else to determine our worth and then we are angry at being under valued."* –Julia Margaret Cameron

The safety and acceptance we believe these external things will bring us, never seem to arrive. It is like chasing the dangling carrot or like a hamster running faster and faster on its wheel thinking it is getting somewhere.

> *"Happiness belongs to those who are sufficient unto themselves. For all external sources of happiness are, by their very nature, highly uncertain, precarious, ephemeral, and subject to change."* –Arthur Schopenhauer

There is nothing wrong or bad about accomplishments and doing things. <u>The question is, are we putting our worth and value as human beings into these things?</u> If we are, does this not create anxiety and fear when we think about the possibility of not getting it? And what happens if we do get it? Are we not going to feel fearful and worry about it being taken away? And if we have our identity tied up in it, how will we feel when it is gone? It will feel as if we are losing a part of ourselves.

Whether it is our money, appearance, job, or significant other we will often go to great measures to hold on to these things out of a fear of loss because that is how we perceive we are receiving our approval, that is how we equate safety, and that is how we are defining our identity.

When our approval comes from another person in a relationship, every little perceived threat makes us feel fearful. We may become jealous and controlling and even angry that this person has so much power over us and our feelings. In some cases, angry to the point of violence.

We are putting our self-worth into the hands of others and asking, "What do you think of me? How do I measure up on your scale?" And we do this to ourselves. That uncomfortable experience of self-consciousness – that big eye we perceive is always following us around, watching us, tormenting us, restricting our freedom.

Whenever we put our approval into the hands of others, we are giving our power away. We feel weak and small, engendering all sorts of feelings – resentment, anger, anxiety, powerlessness, helplessness. Eventually we begin to feel like victims and then blame becomes our coping mechanism.

> ***"When you become immobilized by what anybody else***
> ***thinks of you, what you are saying is that your opinion***
> ***of me is more important than my opinion of myself."*** *–Wayne Dyer*

As long as we retain the hope of reaching this ideal we set for ourselves, we will continue to strive and be motivated – albeit with anxiety, worry, resentment, frustration, and anger. The more shame and lack we feel, the more energy we will expend to fill that lack and to protect that lack from being exposed. But it will never be enough. It will never be enough money, enough power, enough fame, enough accomplishments, enough good looks.

> ***"If God had wanted me otherwise, he would have created me otherwise."***
> *–Johann von Goethe*

Eventually our energy starts to decline. Disappointment after disappointment leads to a diminished hope of ever achieving safety and worthiness – and under that – feelings of peace, freedom, and acceptance. We begin to think that maybe it is just us. Maybe *we* are just stupid or broken or lazy or bad or incompetent and we will always be that way. This belief and feeling begins to permeate our whole being. Every self-conscious moment we punish ourselves for not being good enough. This adds more shame, widening the perceived gap between us and others and sending the cycle spiraling downward. We become harder and harder on ourselves, constantly criticizing. *"God, I'm stupid," "I'm such a loser," "I'm fat," "Get up and do something you lazy bastard," "I'm not a good person."* This critical voice rarely stops, constantly berating us, making us feel worthless. We try to escape with drugs, alcohol, food, shopping, video games, or television to numb the feelings and quiet the mind. But it does not stop.

We feel helpless because we do not know what else to do. We feel we have tried everything or already have everything and it still is not enough. *"Maybe the world just sucks," "Maybe I just suck and that's the way it is and always will be." "That's reality." "Life sucks then you die."* Hope fades fast and so does our energy. The pressure has crushed us. We feel alone and empty and trapped, and life is nothing but dread.

Everything we see is negative and reaffirms our view of our self. We are stuck in this very narrow viewpoint because any attempt at trying something else is feared to lead to another disappointment and add even more shame to our identity.

Now we are depressed and headed down the path toward self-destruction. If the alcohol and drugs do not get us, then suicide might. Our minds chatter away with the voices of judgment and criticism, ranking and comparison. A constant soundtrack of self-debasement. How could we not feel depressed?

Become aware of your expectations.

Becoming aware of our own expectations can help us empathize with others and also aid in preventing or releasing needless pressure we put upon ourselves.

Catch yourself anytime you say the word "should" to yourself or another. It often implies that there is an absolute right way to be or to do something. It is pressure. A demand you place upon yourself. Insert the word "could" and feel the freedom of having or giving a choice.

Positive Expectations

When expectations are formed consciously, without demands or excessive pressure to win approval and respect, they can be quite positive and essential for our individual growth as well as for the health of a society.

Be aware of how advertisers try to influence you. Do not get angry or judgmental about their intentions. You will be giving away your power. They do what they do because we let them. This also does not mean it is wrong or bad to buy their products. Let it be a preference rather than a need.

Notice when you feel overly self-conscious (flushness in the face, fear of eye contact, inhibited actions). You are judging yourself, looking at yourself through the perceived eyes of others. If other people do not like you the way you are and you are not hurting anyone, then it is their problem. You are a unique individual. We are all equal in our worth as humans and we all have different talents, abilities, and intelligences.

Expectation Exercise:

Complete the following sentence stems from a place of feeling. In other words, do them quickly, by-passing the thinking mind.

If only I was more_____, then I could accept myself.

If only I was more_____, then I could accept myself.

If only I was more_____, then I could accept myself.

If only I was more_____, then I could accept myself.

If only I was more_____, then I could accept myself.

If only I was more_____, then I could accept myself.

If only I was _____, then I could accept myself.

If only I was _____, then I could accept myself.

If only I was _____, then I could accept myself.

If only I was _____, then I could accept myself.

If only I was _____, then I could accept myself.

If only I was _____, then I could accept myself.

Complete these sentence stems from that place within that yearns to be loved.

I want to be seen as _____.

I want to be seen as _____.

I want to be seen as _____.

I want to be seen as _____.

I want to be seen as _____.

I want to be seen as _____.

I want to be seen as _____.

I want to be seen as _____.

I want to be seen as _____ .

I want to be seen as _____ .

I don't want to be seen as _____ .

I don't want to be seen as _____ .

I don't want to be seen as _____ .

I don't want to be seen as _____ .

I don't want to be seen as _____ .

I don't want to be seen as _____ .

I don't want to be seen as _____ .

I feel afraid to be seen as _____ .

I feel afraid to be seen as _____ .

I feel afraid to be seen as _____ .

I feel afraid to be seen as _____ .

More often than not, depression is a signal that our current worldview and coping strategies are breaking down and awaiting a new configuration – a new way of perceiving the self, others, and the world – a higher, more complex, more truthful perspective. But, it will not occur until we are willing to open our mind and look within.

Taking the depression call:

"*Time and again people transcend the paralyzing effects of psychological pain when they have sufficient contact with someone who can hear them empathically.*"

—Marshall Rosenberg

Begin by getting their **name and age.**

> *Caller:* "*My name is Sara.*"
> *Listener:* "*And how old are you, Sara?*"
> *Caller:* "*29.*"

Listener: "29. What's going on tonight? You sound kind of down."

Ask **Open-Ended questions** to gather the <u>Big Picture</u>. Make sure you **Reflect** back their feelings and do **Perception Checking** in order to understand them accurately.

Caller: *"Yeah. I've been real low on energy lately."*
Listener: *"And how long have you been feeling low on energy?"*
Caller: *"I guess a few months now. But it's getting worse."*
Listener: *"A couple of months, huh? Tell me about how it's getting worse."*

Ask about **specific complaints** and **trigger events**. Let them tell us about what is going on in their life and how they are feeling to gather the **Big Picture**.

Caller: *"I've just been crying all the time and not eating very much and . . ."*

Summarize back to a caller when they give us large chunks information.

Listener: *"So let me make sure I've got all this. You have been crying a lot and not eating or sleeping well. You hardly leave the house and are having trouble concentrating and remembering. And this has been going on for a couple of months. Is this accurate?"*

Caller: *"Yeah I just can't get myself together."*

Listener: *"You sound frustrated about your situation."*

Caller: *"Yes. Extremely frustrated."*

Listener: *"What do you think may have triggered all these feelings?"*

At some point we will want to **explore** any significant friends and family in their life as well as their current work or school situation.

Listener: *"Who else have you spoken to about your feelings?"*

Caller: *"No one. I would be way too embarrassed to tell anyone."*

Listener: *"Well, I'm glad you called here tonight. Just talking about your feelings is an important first step to feeling better."*

Whenever feelings are discussed that the caller is uncomfortable about, it is effective to ***Validate and Normalize*** *those feelings.*

Listener: *"I can only imagine how hard this has been for you. It is not uncommon for people to feel this way given these circumstances."*

Listener: *"It's really okay to feel angry."*

Ask the caller about any **pressures or expectations** they feel in their life. How do they feel about themselves? Explore any *anger* they may be feeling, but do not force the issue if they resist. Many depressed people will deny feeling angry because stuffing down the anger and turning it upon themselves is their current coping mechanism. They may feel great anger toward certain people but also believe they cannot survive without them. Therefore, they turn the anger inward and accuse and condemn themselves without much empathy and compassion. Our job is to show them the empathy and compassion they aren't giving to themselves and to do this no matter what they are feeling.

After we have gathered the Big Picture and have agreed what path to focus on, we can move into **Problem Solving**. Keep asking open-ended questions, reflect and perception check consistently, and be empathic, warm, and non-judgmental.

Explore any hopes, dreams, and desires they may have. Then discuss possible action steps they can take in that direction.

> Listener: *"If you could start all over again and do anything you wanted without any pressure or judgment, what would it be?"*

> Listener: *"What do you like to do?" "What would you like to do?" "How would you like to feel?"*

Remember, *we* are not going to be solving *their* problems. Ask them what *they* have tried or want to try. Explore all feelings toward these efforts. Later, we can offer some of our own suggestions. Avoid saying *"you should," "you need to,"* or *"you ought to."* And definitely do not give advice.

Resources and Referrals

We always recommend that people suffering from depression seek some form of professional counseling. Other referrals and suggestions we can offer include: support groups, journaling, volunteering, reading self-help, spiritual, or psychology books, exercise and yoga, nutrition, meditation and relaxation exercises.

It is not unusual to discover that people suffering from a depression are also being treated with antidepressant medication. Medication is effective for the severely depressed, but if not taken along side some sort of therapy, then lasting changes are improbable, and the person will become dependent upon this medication to feel balanced.

<u>Towards a Deeper Understanding . . .</u>

Resistance

**"We don't move away from real pain; we move away from
what we believe will lead to pain."** *–Anthony Robbins.*

Depressed people hold a lot of negative beliefs about the self and the future. Often these beliefs and outlooks are seen as "realistic." "*I'm just being realistic.*" Do not tell them they are wrong. It won't work. The *known* misery may feel safer than anything *unknown*, therefore people may be resistant to any suggestions, change, risks, or new ways of thinking. A part of them wants to feel better yet another part is fearful of getting hopes up and being disappointed and hurt again. Set aside your own frustration and helplessness and instead, be relentless with your patience and empathy. And be consistent with your encouragement.

Reflect and empathize with feelings of fear, and if necessary gently invite the caller to consider that without even small risk there is no chance to change.

> *Listener:* *"I know change seems difficult. In fact, sometimes it feels impossible. It can be scary, but sometimes it is necessary, if we want to stop feeling so bad. And I want you to know that I'm here to help you."*

> *Listener:* *"It sounds like there is a part of you that wants to feel better, try new things, and another part of you doesn't believe that is safe – to get your hopes up again. Is that accurate?"*

Powerlessness

**"You can have no inner peace as long as the controls
of your life are located outside of yourself."** *–Wayne Dyer*

There is a profound sense of being out of control for the depressed person. Even the smallest perceived change can bring up dread and overwhelm. Panic attacks and outbursts of anger are common. Their critical mind beats them down and makes them feel helpless in a world perceived to be against them. Often the depressed caller will transfer responsibility onto the counselor, asking for advice and wanting the counselor to give them all the answers.

The depressed person wants more than healing. They often want everything back. A magical restoration of everything the way it once was. They may have certain expectations of help from us, which we cannot provide. This may engender feelings of guilt within us and frustration for not being able to do more.[1] Remember, we do what we can. Our chief job is to use our basic skills, empathize, and offer referrals. We are not here to fix, change, heal, or rescue them.

Callers will often have two conflicting voices in their head. One that wants to take risks and another that seeks security. This conflict may go around and around, back and forth, wearing a person down, eventually immobilizing them. We can help the caller to express both voices, trying to uncover what each perspective hopes for and is afraid of. Hearing both sides can help the caller become aware that they have a choice. And through the expression of these feelings, emotional blockages can dissipate and move out.[2]

Empowerment

Empowering a caller is supporting them with getting in touch with their own problem solving abilities. It is appropriate at times for us to be challenging and persistent in getting callers to think of ways they could begin to cope better. Often, *discussing all their choices, their feelings and thoughts about each choice, and the possible consequences of each choice helps them to sort things out.* Uncovering past situations in which they successfully coped with difficult situations can also give a caller some confidence to deal in the here and now.

Be authentic

Often we will attempt to be overly friendly with the depressed person. The caller may end up feeling worse because they feel they cannot return the friendliness. This may be a signal that you are trying to cheer them up – a subtle attempt to try to change or fix them. Just notice these desires without self-judgment, and then move into the knowing that they are perfect just as they are. When you can allow yourself and others to be just as they are – you are being fully authentic.

EMPATHY DEVELOPMENT

Awareness #2

As human beings, we all feel, we all suffer.

We have all been wounded.
We have all been hurt.

We have all felt the anger of being treated unfairly.
We have all felt revengeful.   And resentful.
And we certainly all feel sadness.

We all feel frustration when we can't seem to get what we want.
We all feel disappointment when things don't turn out the way we wished.

We all feel afraid from time to time.
We have all worried about what is coming next.

We have all felt alone.
We have all felt abandoned.   And rejected.   And unloved.

We all hide to some degree.
We have all felt humiliated and embarrassed.
We have all felt bad.
Most of us have felt pessimistic, cynical, and depressed at some point too.

We have all felt the agony of great loss.

We have all felt not good enough.
And we have all pushed ourselves way too hard.

We have all felt misunderstood.
Victimized.
Trapped.

We have all felt overwhelmed.
We have all been afraid of losing control.

Most of us have felt confused, lost, or hopeless.
Many of us have felt great despair.

We all want to feel safe. We all want to fit in.
We are all afraid to die. Many of us have wanted to die.

All of us yearn to be loved . . . to be free . . . to be at peace . . .

to be released from this suffering . . .
and we don't know how.

I have too.

I can recognize it in you because I know it in me.
I can relate.
I know how it feels.

I understand that it hurts.
And I care.

To the degree we can recognize and be with feelings and desires in ourselves, without judgment, without trying to get rid of them, or without trying to change them, is the degree to which we can accept them in another. It is the depth at which we are able to accept the full range of the human experience that determines the depth at which we are able to empathize with another.

Empathy and Depression

> *"Depression is nourished by a lifetime of ungrieved*
> *and unforgiven hurts"* –Penelope Sweet

Journal on the times in your life that you felt depressed. What were your feelings? In what ways did you feel lacking? What were some of your symptoms? Behaviors? What would you have wanted from someone during this time?

Be aware that much of depression comes out of self-hatred and shame for not living up to internalized expectations.

Notice any frustration you feel toward a person's negative beliefs and resistance to change. Change is scary because they truly believe they have tried everything and that more attempts will just result in more failure and more pain. Notice any discomfort you have toward their feelings and be aware of trying to cheer them up, fix, or rescue them.

> *"The things about people that drive us crazy are the things*
> *that are keeping them sane."* –On Becoming a Counselor

Empathize with all of a person's feelings as well as your own feelings. Listen and hear the deeper message these feelings are communicating. Most upset feelings spring from shame and hurt. When we shame feelings such as fear, sadness, and anger, we add more shame, judgment, and hurt, and actually make these feelings stronger. Only through acceptance can we grow, heal, and make new choices.

GRIEF – DEATH and DYING

"Death is never a singular event. In addition to the
actual death, there is the death of all the hopes, dreams,
and expectations about the future." –Grief Recovery Handbook

Whether it is the break up of a relationship, the loss of a job, the death of a significant loved one, or a terminal illness, issues of loss are all too common to counselors.

Grief is the conflicting group of human emotions caused by an end to or change in a familiar pattern of behavior.[12] It is a natural, continuing, and individual reaction to loss. As the body requires time from a physical injury, one's emotional life needs time to recover from loss. Each person's responses to a loss are unique, but some of the more common grieving responses are:

- A deep sense of sadness, crying.
- Tightness in throat or heaviness in chest, breathlessness.
- Empty feeling in stomach and loss of appetite.
- Lack of energy and weakness in muscles.
- Shock and/or numbness – lack of feeling.
- Helplessness.
- Relief (particularly if loved one suffered a lengthy or painful illness).
- Guilt.
- Anger (at themselves, or at loved one for things they did or didn't do and for leaving them).
- Restlessness, difficulty concentrating and sleeping.
- Mood changes.
- Feeling as if the loss isn't real, that it did not actually happen.
- Sensing the loved one's presence.
- Assuming mannerisms or traits of the deceased.
- Experiencing an intense preoccupation with the life of the deceased.
- Needing to talk and remember things about the deceased.

These are all natural and normal grief responses. As a telephone crisis specialist, it is important to express this to a caller. Normalize their feelings. Many times a person who is grieving feels like they are going crazy. As listeners we need to be willing to hear them cry and express their feelings.

So often, people respond to the grieving person with emotional dismissing phrases like: *"Don't feel bad," "Don't cry," "You'll find somebody else," "Time heals all wounds," "Be strong," "Keep busy, it'll take your mind off of it,"* and *"They just need to be alone for a while."* These statements tell the person not to feel what they are feeling, to deny their pain, to immediately start replacing the loss, and to deal with the loss alone. None of these responses will help the person work through the grieving process in a healthy manner.

Grieving and mourning are inescapable. They may be postponed, side-stepped, avoided, or denied but eventually this process seeks expression and influences behavior. The longer it is denied and avoided, the more difficult it is to deal with.

Some of the major tasks of mourning include:

- Accepting the reality of the loss.
- Working through the pain of grief.
- Adjusting to an environment without the deceased.
- Moving on with life.

The bereaved must often come to terms with living alone, raising children alone, facing an empty house, and managing finances alone. The reshaping of one's personal identity and the revising of personal relationships are also part of the adjustment process.

It is impossible to set a definitive date for this mourning process to be accomplished. One sign of a completed grief reaction is when the person is able to think about the deceased without pain. There is always a sense of sadness, but it lacks that wrenching quality it had before. Also, mourning is finished when a person can reinvest emotions back into life and living.[5]

Some causes of complicated Grief:

--*If the bereaved was overly dependent.* The deceased may have been their main source of approval and safety. They might feel terrified to be on their own and feel like they have lost a major part of themselves.

--*The manner of death.* Sudden death, multiple losses, suicides, homicides, AIDS deaths, drug overdoses, or ambiguous losses, such as missing persons may cause so much confusion and distress that the mourner may not be able to manage a normal grief reaction.

--*History of depression.* If the bereaved is depressed or has a history of being depressed, it can make it more difficult for the person to cope adequately.

Some common symptoms of a complicated grief process:

- Unable to talk about the deceased, even after years.
- Withdrawal from relationships and activities for an extended time.
- Keeping the house or the room of the deceased the same (denial).

Depression is not a natural part of grieving, but it is quite prevalent nonetheless. Therefore, it is considered normal. The major difference between normal grieving and depression is that the grieving person does not allow the loss to affect his or her self-worth. When the two are combined (low self-worth and a significant loss), the grieving process can become much more difficult. A major loss can reawaken this negative set of beliefs about the self.

Unfinished business with a major loss can start with an examination of what the caller feels **could have done better, more, or different in the relationship.**

The Grief Recovery Handbook offers the helpful suggestion of **writing a letter** to the deceased or person separated from. The letter will not be sent but will be used for a sense of emotional expression and closure.

Start the letter off with:

> *I want to tell you . . .*
> *I apologize for . . .*
> *I forgive you for . . .*
> *I want you to know* . . . (significant emotional statements and
> *undelivered* communication).

End the letter with:

> *I love you. I miss you. Good bye.*

It can also help to read this letter to someone else. Preferably someone who is a good listener.

Stages of the Terminally Ill and the Bereaved.

While dying is the ultimate loss experience, the stages that the terminal patient passes through provide broad guidelines for understanding all loss as well as the grieving process. In her ground breaking work, *On Death and Dying*, Elisabeth Kubler-Ross outlined the stages of the dying patient which have profoundly influenced the treatment of those suffering terminal illness.

Denial
The fact of one's impending death is experienced as unreal and impossible. One may avoid talking about it or not allow others to mention it. Denial is a defense that allows the person to cope. Do not push them out of this stage. It is considered therapeutically unwise and generally unkind to do so.

The dying person, sensing the discomfort of others, may avoid talking about themselves, their condition, or their fate out of sensitivity to others or to prevent an even greater fear – abandonment.

Anger

Dying patients often rage at their impending death. They may be angry with God, their family, themselves, or anyone who is healthy and takes their life for granted. No one is exempt from their anger no matter how close or how good you may have been to the dying person. Being able to uncritically accept the anger without judgment helps the person express all of these important feelings. Let them vent.

Bargaining

Patients may try to make bargains with doctors, caretakers, God, themselves, in an attempt to postpone death. *"Let me just . . . and then I'll go quietly."* They want to buy time, to finish something, to make amends. Family members may feel this way too if they also have some unresolved issues.

Anticipatory Grief

The dying person is losing everyone and everything they have ever loved and cherished in life. It is a formidable task accompanied by enormous sadness and grief. It is a time of release and "good-byes." It can be a quiet time, turning inward, thinking about the meaning of their life. Words and conversation make way for silent togetherness. This is a hard time for the helper since there is nothing to be done except to be present.

Acceptance

For some, death is a defeat; a battle fought and lost. For others, death becomes an integral part of life. A natural end to the life experience. Acceptance breeds a peacefulness and composure. Just being present with the person is the most important thing you can do.

Avoid trying to move anyone through these stages. Not everyone goes through all the stages and some may not go through them in this order. These stages are a useful framework for thinking about how people handle any and all losses.

Taking the Grief Call:

Listening while **Validating and Normalizing feelings is the most important thing one can do to help the grieving person.** Do not try to get them to replace the loss or isolate themselves, and do not attempt to intellectualize their emotions with phrases like *"He's in a better place," "All things must pass," "She led a full life."* Remember, grieving people want and need to be heard, not fixed.

A great question is always, *"What can I do for you right now?"* or *"How can I best support you right now?"*

Offering referrals to counselors, support groups, or any other agencies that could be of further assistance is always encouraged. Get to know which agencies offer this kind of support. Help them cope, find support, and deal with unfinished business. *Get them through the night.*

Empathy: Death and Dying

"If we become skilled in giving ourselves empathy,
we often experience in just a few seconds a natural release of energy
that enables us to be present with the other person." **–Marshall Rosenberg**

Journal on all the feelings you experienced when you suffered a significant loss in your life – sadness, guilt, anger, fear, shock, etc. What would you have wanted from someone during that time?

Notice any discomfort you have in discussing death and dying.

Journal on the beliefs about death you hold that engenders this fear and discomfort.

Notice any feelings or urges you have to try and push your beliefs about death, life, and afterlife on another.

Empathize with the anger, guilt and other feelings a person has in response to their loss. Everyone, given their life circumstances, has a reason for feeling the way they do. Let them express their feelings in an environment of acceptance at their own pace and the healing will take place.

Notice any feelings of helplessness or powerlessness you feel when trying to help a person deal with their own impending and inevitable death. This may manifest as a desire to save or get the person out of fear and sadness. It could also show up as frustration and anger if the person resists your efforts to save them.

EMPATHY DEVELOPMENT

Releasing our Judgments
Exercise #2

<u>Judgments are the biggest barrier to empathy.</u>

<u>The first step is to become aware of what our judgments are.</u>

<u>The second step is to become aware of why we judge.</u>

In exercise one, you observed your judgments and wrote down the five qualities that seemed to upset you the most. For this exercise, write down those five qualities in the left column. In the right column, write the opposite quality.

e.g . . . . . *laziness*   opposite . . . . . *hard working or motivated.*
e.g . . . . . *selfishness*   opposite . . . . . *selflessness*

1._____ opposite _____

2._____ opposite _____

3._____ opposite _____

4._____ opposite _____

5._____ opposite _____

How many of these opposite traits do you believe describe you? Which ones?

_____

Have you ever expressed any of the qualities that upset you? List some examples of each. This might take some digging. You may also search for ways you express these qualities with yourself. (e.g. critical of yourself; judging itself can be considered selfish, lazy thinking, arrogant).

_____

_____

_____

Could you find examples for some qualities but not others? Which ones could you not?

In reality, we are every quality.

Why do we deny and judge certain qualities within ourselves and try so hard to express others?

Like our internalized expectations, our judgments are formed in childhood based on our parents' and society's beliefs about what is good and what is bad. "Good" qualities got expressed. "Bad" ones got disowned and repressed.

When we judge a quality and then disown it, we erect a *boundary* on our wholeness – split ourselves into parts – good parts and bad parts. This creates a painful wound. Next we begin our task of protecting ourselves from being hurt again. Anxiety forms to keep us internally and externally vigilant of signs of this "bad" part. The bad parts become exiled, hidden away, "not me," and then we form an opposite quality (a protective part) that "is me" in which we spend an enormous amount of energy to express and exhibit.

So fearful we are of expressing this bad "not me" quality, that we *shame it* and even *deny it* out of our own identity. But it does not go away. A shamed quality will express itself whether we like it or not. More than likely in an unhealthy manner. And how could it not? It believes it is bad, defective, and evil.

The harder we push the shamed quality down, the more *pressure* builds up within. But this energy needs release and it often seeps out, and sometimes explodes out, in backdoor ways.

Some good examples of this are:
- Priests who deny sexual thoughts and then molest children.
- Anti-abortionists, who are against killing a life, then bomb a clinic (killing doctors).
- People who complain about people who complain.
- Judging people who judge people (watch out for that one).

If my parents were super critical and judgmental of every mistake that I made, and I internalized this to mean that I am stupid, then I would do anything I could to be seen as perfect and smart all the time. If I were to be seen as stupid or incompetent, I would be afraid of being judged again as well as fearful of losing my parents' love and caretaking. To a child or child part within us, it can feel like our very survival is at stake.

But no matter how hard I try to be seen as smart and competent, underneath this persona I wear in the world is a feeling that I am stupid and incompetent. It continues to sit there, out of my awareness, yet driving my behavior to be perfect or competent at all times. I will be critical of others and their intelligence. I may act like a know-it-all or an expert. I may be extremely sensitive to criticism or feedback from others – it may touch that spot of hurt – that wound within me, and immediately my defenses go up and I react with anger. *The harsher my reaction, the stronger the denial, the deeper the wound.*

As soon as we disown an aspect, the universe then goes to work by bringing forward people and situations that embody this judged quality, often to the extreme, to give us the opportunity to reown it and move into balance and wholeness. The physical indicator of judgment is *tension*, and the emotional signal is *anger or irritation.*

We are giving our power away when we judge. Every time someone says or does that thing we consider bad, we react with anger. It is as if they are pushing our buttons. This button of ours that is being pushed is a *point of pain* – a wound – a shame spot. An exiled "not me" part of us that was *labeled and punished* as bad at some point in our life.

By becoming aware of our denied qualities and reowning them *in a healthy way*, we are adding energy and vitality to our lives. We are no longer using up our energy defending and protecting ourselves all of the time. We reduce the conflict we experience with others. We are also developing empathy, because we now accept and embrace those previously judged qualities.

The results of integration will be:

More energy.	Less fatigue.
More freedom of choice.	Less feeling like a victim.
More power and control.	Less anxiety & manipulation.
More peace/acceptance.	Less reactivity and/or anger.
More empathy	Less judgment and conflict.

The next Judgment exercise will focus on how to *reinterpret* and integrate our denied qualities.

Discernment versus Reactive Judgments

Word of caution – do not throw the baby out with the bathwater in regards to judgments. We are talking about releasing *reactive judgments* here – judgments that label someone as bad and cause us some degree of upset. These are not to be confused with *discerning judgments.* Discernment is the wisdom, knowledge, and ability to make choices based on what works and what doesn't. It is neutral and non-reactive, and it uses keen insight to choose the higher, wider, and deeper in our lives. Without this ability, our growth is stunted.

SEX AND SEXUALITY

Since we were kids we have been taught that sex is a kind of taboo subject matter. Many of us have been conditioned to believe that sex is dirty and shameful, even though sex is undoubtedly a normal and natural human act in all cultures since the beginning of time. These mixed messages are confusing to people, and especially confusing to adolescents who are trying to form their identities.

Even though the taboo of sex is slowly lifting in many first world cultures, there still remains a feeling that it is shameful to have sex, talk about it, or even think about it.

The entertainment and advertisement industries help perpetuate these mixed messages while a gigantic pornography industry thrives upon it.

Issues surrounding sex and sexuality are often fraught with our own personal biases, and most of us carry strong opinions about these issues. It is hard to imagine someone not having an opinion on abortion or having some feelings regarding homosexuality. Calls concerning these matters often require us to dig deeper into our empathy, putting our personal feelings and judgments aside.

This section will cover not just sexual behavior but also some of the potential consequences of sexual behavior – pregnancy, abortion, and STDs. It will also encompass issues of sexuality – homosexuality, gender-identity, and other sexual variations.

Being informed about the different issues surrounding sex and sexuality will aid you in understanding, educating, and making appropriate referrals and suggestions. This manual only covers a basic knowledge of the sexual concerns people with be calling about. For more information, it is recommended that you seek out other, more in depth sources.

Pregnancy
After delivering a child, roughly half of all new mothers experience what is known as the "**maternity blues**." Symptoms include weeping, depression, irritability, shifting moods, tension, and anger, but typically only lasts a few days and are more common in first births than in subsequent ones.

A woman who, after giving birth, wishes that she never had a child or that she truly cannot be an adequate parent, may be suffering from **postpartum depression**. Symptoms involve extreme *sadness, apathy, despair, and worthlessness*. She also may feel extremely *guilty* that she is not thrilled with her "new addition." With medical attention, these women often overcome their symptoms and can become loving, attentive parents. Without treatment, the mother and child risk future abuse and neglect.

With any call involving pregnancy, we are dealing with feelings – *the caller's feelings.* We are not medical doctors and we do not give advice based on what we think they should do. The only way to be sure (or unsure) of pregnancy is to take a reliable test, preferably by a medical technician. Those who are calling us for information about what to expect, how to care for their fetus, etc. should be referred to a medical setting.

We listen, empathize, gather the Big Picture, and help them to sort out their choices while making a plan that is right for *them.*

Menopause

Menopause is when women cease to have reproductive functioning. It typically occurs between the ages of 45 and 55. This phase generally lasts for about fifteen years and involves a slow decrease in fertility and other bodily changes – most noticeably in bone density, thinning of the hair, weight gain, decreased flexibility, mood swings, in addition to the well-known "hot flashes." Some women may experience a decrease in sexual desire and vaginal lubrication, while others discover a new found freedom from the constant concerns of birth control and menstruation.

Estrogen production diminishes during this time and some women opt for hormone replacement therapy. Although estrogen is correlated with a reduction in heart disease, it also comes with an increase risk of cancer. There are several new options for women and we should refer them to speak with their medical doctor. Women are advised to do regular breast self-exams and receive yearly mammograms.

Again, we do not give medical advice in these matters, but rather listen, empathize, get the Big Picture, and help them to sort out choices.

Birth Control

Birth control refers to the *active* prevention of pregnancy. The ways of preventing pregnancy fall into several categories:

- *Natural methods* include abstinence (not having sex at all) and the "rhythm method." This last technique involves a woman monitoring her body temperature to determine the time of ovulation and avoiding sex during that time. It is a tricky method and has a low effectiveness rate. Withdrawal involves pulling the penis out of the vagina before ejaculation. It has a low effectiveness rate.

- *Surgical methods.* Men may undergo a vasectomy where the tubes that carry sperm from the testicles are cut and sealed off in the scrotum. Women must have an operation (tubal ligation) to cut and seal off the Fallopian tubes connecting the ovaries which release the eggs and the uterus. People who are looking for a permanent way to prevent birth turn to these methods.

- *Barrier methods* include the use of condoms to cover the penis and prevent semen from entering the woman's body, and a diaphragm (88% effective) inserted into the vagina to block the semen from entering the uterus. There is also a female condom that is inserted into the vagina up to eight hours before having sex. These are very effective especially if used with a chemical method. *The birth control sponge* is inserted deep into the vagina before sex. It is made of soft, squishy plastic, covers the cervix, and contains spermicide to help prevent pregnancy.

- *Chemical methods* involve the use of creams, foams and jellies that contain chemicals that kill sperm in the woman's body. They are usually used with another method of birth control because alone they have a very low effectiveness rate. Other chemical methods include:

  - *The birth control pill* prevents the production of eggs by creating levels of estrogen and progesterone that mimic pregnancy. When used correctly (every day), this method is very effective.

  - *The birth control ring* (NuvaRing) is a small, flexible ring that is worn inside the vagina releasing hormones to stop ovulation and prevent pregnancy.

  - *Birth control implant*: Nexplanon is a matchstick-size, flexible rod implanted under the skin in the upper arm that releases the hormone progestin steadily and prevents pregnancy for up to four years. It is 99% effective. If you change your mind, you can have your doctor remove it. Nexplanon does not prevent STDs.

  - *The birth control patch* or transdermal contraceptive patch releases hormones that prevents pregnancy. It is worn on the skin, replaced every week for three weeks, then you get a week off before you repeat the cycle. It is considered safe and affordable.

  - *The birth control shot* (Depo-Provera) is an injection you get from a physician or nurse once every three months. It's considered safe, convenient, and effective if you always get it on time.

- *One other method is the intrauterine device or IUD.* This is a small object placed in the uterus by a physician to prevent pregnancy. It continually irritates the lining of the womb so that the pregnancy never really begins. If a woman wants to become pregnant later, it can be removed in a doctor's office. It has a 99% effectiveness rate.

Help the caller sort out all of their choices and the possible consequences and risks with each one. If you do not know the information they are asking, do not pretend that you do. Refer them to an agency that does. Then seek out information so that you will be better informed the next time you take a similar call.

Abortion

Terminating a pregnancy can be done by several methods. Most commonly, a doctor in his or her office or clinic will open the cervix (opening of the uterus) and insert an instrument that vacuums out the fertilized egg and the thickened lining of the uterus. Once complete, the woman is no longer pregnant. There are also chemical agents that can be given by mouth or injected, which cause the termination of a pregnancy. With any method of abortion, the woman must watch for excessive bleeding afterwards and see a doctor immediately if bleeding continues.

Controversy continues over the performing of abortions in the US, especially so-called late-term abortions, when the fetus is more developed and may have a chance of survival outside the womb. Abortion is a personal and political issue which some see as the murder of an unborn child while others view it as a viable means of avoiding an unwanted pregnancy and a matter of personal freedom for women.

The experience of having an abortion or even considering ending a pregnancy can be a source of emotional stress for a woman, her family and the father of the unborn baby. There may be *confusion* over the decision to abort or offering the child up for adoption. There may also be *regret* over either of these decisions.

Women and men who have lost a pregnancy due to **miscarriage** may go through an extended grieving process. In particular, women who have miscarried may harbor feelings of *guilt and shame*. They may feel that they did something to cause the situation, or that they are somehow less of a woman because they could not sustain the pregnancy. Of course, for those whom the miscarriage was a positive event, there may be no grieving process at all and these individuals may actually be much more relieved than grieved.

When a person mentions a recent miscarriage, make sure to ask the caller how *they* are feeling before jumping to any premature conclusions.

If a caller requests a referral to a clinic that gives abortions and this violates your personal beliefs, we are obligated to give this information without questioning motives.

We listen, empathize, get the Big Picture, and guide the caller toward choices, information, and resources that will enable them to make an informed decision.

Infertility

Finding out one is infertile and cannot bear children can be excruciatingly painful for a person. A sense of being defective may create fears of abandonment by their partner. Men often take it as a shot against their masculinity. For some it is a loss of immortality, a carrying on of their genes, of themselves, of their dreams and expectations. Feelings of anger and depression may ensue.

Infertility treatments can quickly deplete financial resources putting even more stress on the couple.

Explore all of their feelings with empathy. Normalize, Validate, Perception Check, and Reflect.

STDs (Sexually Transmitted Diseases)

Statistics:
According to the Centers for Disease Control and Prevention (2016)[11]
- 20 million new cases of STDs are diagnosed each year.
- More than half of new cases are young people between 15-24.
- Reported cases of STDs have been on the rise since 2006.

Sexually transmitted diseases are, as the name implies, transmitted through sexual contact. STDs present a particular problem, as many are virtually undetectable and some people do not even realize they have one. Even when people do know that they have an STD, many will not share this information with their partner for *fear of being rejected.*

Some of the more common STDs include Gonorrhea (the Clap), Syphilis, Chlamydia, Herpes, Hepatitis, Genital warts, and Crabs. Sores, rashes, a burning sensation when urinating, and more serious complications can occur if left untreated. The viruses spread mainly through genital, oral, or anal contact. Some can be spread by other means.

STDs can profoundly impact intimate relationships and may force women to reconsider their ability (or desire to) have children. In addition, many *feel damaged and/or angry* toward those who have infected them. Others seek out partners who also suffer from the disease to avoid having to explain or justify their symptoms.

"Safe-sex" practices are essential to limiting the spread of STDs and for many the rigors of safe sex are by-passed in the heat of the moment. Safe sex involves communicating with your partner openly and honestly. Talk about sex and your sexual histories. Know your partner.[5]

> ***"While the transmission of an STD can take only seconds, the
> effects can last a lifetime."***

Many callers want to know if they have an STD or what to do if they get one, and while these are useful questions, we are not medical practitioners. Listen, empathize, and provide information, referrals, and choices to help them make an informed decision.

HIV/AIDS

Statistics:
According to the organization UNAIDS:[13]
- As of 2016, an estimated 36.7 million people worldwide were living with HIV/AIDS, including 1.8 million children.
- Approximately 30% of these people don't know they have the disease.
- Approximately 35 million people globally have died from AIDS (1 million in 2016).

According to the Centers for Disease Control and Prevention:[11]
- In the U.S., as of 2014, approximately 1.2 million people have HIV/AIDS.
- New cases in the United States are down 18% between 2008 and 2014.

Acquired Immune Deficiency Syndrome (AIDS) is a viral disease which nearly destroys the body's immune system. The result is a life-threatening illness resulting from any of a number of infections.

The Causative virus is the Human Immunodeficiency Virus (HIV). This virus lives in blood, semen, and to a lesser extent in other body fluids. Once passed into another person's bloodstream by sex, sharing of needles for injecting drugs, or by blood transfusions, it takes hold infecting the new host. After about three months, it can be detected by a blood test or a test of a swab from the inside of the mouth. There is no definitive cure but new drugs and antiretroviral therapy are helping those with HIV to live longer and get fewer infections.

An AIDS call can involve a number of different feelings – *denial, anger, fear, depression, sadness, guilt, rage, and shame*. There may also be feelings of *hopelessness and thoughts of suicide*. Learning to live with the disease can be an experience fraught with *confusion* over who one is now, while all of the person's relationships will be affected to some degree if and when the illness is disclosed.

Listen, Normalize and Validate all of the caller's feelings. *Notice any judgments* you may be feeling and then choose to look deeper. Empathize with the pain and feelings of this person. **Reflect** back these feelings and help the caller to sort out all the choices available to them. If they feel there is no hope and are contemplating suicide, you will have to take the call in a different direction (refer to the suicide section of this manual).

Legal Notes
Normally, young people under the age of 18 must have a parent or guardian's permission to get health care. The law allows minors to seek care for pregnancy, birth control, or STDs without such consent in some states. For callers who want to seek these kinds of services but are afraid their parents must know, we can assure them that the law protects their privacy in these matters. However, we may also explore their relationship with their parents and support system during this stressful time.

Paraphilias

There are a wide variety of sexual behaviors that may be practiced – some traditional or at least usual – others not so much. We need to be somewhat desensitized to some of these non-traditional sexual behaviors so that we will not be shocked when a caller discusses these activities.

Some people feel the need to do certain things in order to be sexually aroused, others simply prefer them, still others choose to experiment from time to time (or only once) with something new. Do not assume.

Certain unusual sexual practices are grouped together under the term "paraphilias."

- *Fetishes* – sexual arousal from an object such as a boot or undergarment.
- *Pedophilia* – attraction to pre-adolescent boys or girls.
- *Frotteurism* – rubbing up against someone, often a stranger in a public place.
- *Voyeurism* – secretly watching someone.
- *Exhibitionism* – exposing oneself to an often unsuspecting person.
- *Sexual Masochism and Sexual Sadism* – a continuum of sexual behaviors that involve the combination of pleasure and pain.

The activity may be harmful in that it puts the person in legal danger (some of these activities are illegal), and that it creates a barrier to forming a deep, loving, intimate relationship with another adult. We, as listeners, may be called upon to put these experiences in perspective for the caller. *Explore the caller's feelings about the consequences of his or her behavior.* Do they want to stop? Is it creating a distance between the caller and his/her significant other? What does it give them? What does it cost them?

These calls can often bring up some of our strongest judgments. We must be vigilant in our consciousness to make the discernment between the person and their behaviors. We do not have to like their behaviors or condone them, but the truth is that people are more than their behaviors, *and* they are doing the best they can given their level of awareness and their life conditions (including their past). So we empathize, listen, work to understand the deeper motives, meanings, and wants, and then explore together new choices if they are open and willing.

If the caller is engaged in sexual behavior with a minor, this is a reportable act. Please see the Child Abuse section of this manual for more information.

Sexual Orientation and Gender Identity

Gender is social construct, an idea created by people to help categorize and explain the world around them. A distinction is made between sex (male/female) which is a biological given at birth, and gender (man/woman) which is a sociological and psychological construction concerned with characteristics that are not biological.

Each gender comes with a set of expectations, such as how to act, feel, dress, talk, interact with others. We learn what it means to be a man or woman, boy or girl at a very early age from parents, friends, culture, religion, media, and more. The list of expectations varies at different stages of development and across cultures.

We should become comfortable talking to people whose sexual orientation and gender identity are different from our own. On the crisis line, our place is not to judge, only to help callers deal with their feelings and attain the support they need. Never label your caller. Let them pick the label if they choose.

While progress is being made in regards to acceptance, openness, empathy, and fair treatment for people of non-mainstream sexual orientations and gender identities in our culture, there continues to be a strong stigma. People who fall into this category often experience judgment and discrimination from others for being sinful, dirty, sick, wrong, broken, confused, bad. They may feel shame, guilt, anger, lonely, sad, afraid, alienated, hopeless, trapped. A large amount of energy and time may be devoted to defense and hiding rather than to intimacy and growth. The public self may become a form of disguise and armor, with the private self consequently becoming increasingly alienated from the rest of the world, leading to a sense of shame about one's core identity and basic needs.[5]

Statistics show that teens who are gay are seven times more likely to commit suicide than their non-gay peers. Suicide attempts among transgender individuals are as high as 41% over the course of a lifetime. This is in comparison to the national rate of 4.2% (over the course of lifetime).[14]

LGBTQ is an acronym that stands for Lesbian, Gay, Bisexual, Trans and Queer. Different organizations may use fewer or more letters, for example, an 'I' to indicate Intersex people.

Despite the definitions and labels listed below, it is important to honor each individual's right to self-define into any or none of the categories below.

Lesbian: A woman who is attracted to other women.

Gay: A man who is attracted to other men.

Bisexual: An individual who is attracted to both genders.

Transgender: An umbrella term that describes individuals whose gender identities do not match their biological sex, for example, somebody who is born male-bodied and identifies as a woman. Transgender is also an umbrella term that encompasses other labels such as genderqueer and gender non-conforming.

Queer: Individuals who experience fluidity in their experience of sexuality or gender and therefore do not identify strictly as LGB or T. The term 'Queer' can also include those who do not identify as either gender. They may avoid gender-specific pronouns like "she/her" and he/him" and use more neutral pronouns instead.

Asexual individuals, also known as "Ace" or "Aces," often desire emotional intimate relationships but may have little or no interest in having sex. They come from any gender, age, or background. They may have a spouse and/or children. They may be attracted to both men and women.

Pansexual (pan) is used to describe a person who is attracted to all types of people, no matter their sex or gender.

Intersex: An individual who is born with biological characteristics of both sexes.

Transvestite describes someone who wears the clothing of the opposite sex for sexual arousal. Most often they are heterosexual men who enjoy wearing women's clothing.

Be sure to be curious and ask questions using perception checking to discover what each label means to each person. Empower people to identify in the way that feels best to them. Don't rush a caller into coming up with an answer. There is no wrong way to identify, and it is okay to be uncertain.

Coming Out: A How-To

The process of coming to terms with one's own sexual orientation or gender identity and then telling friends and family is called "coming out (of the closet)." It is a long process of self-discovery, uncertainty, pain and ideally soul-searching, friend-finding and strength. People are at various stages of coming out at different times in their lives. **Never pressure a caller to come out as** *they* **must be ready to do so.** It can be a lonely process, and our compassion and empathy can be of real help.

Revealing an important part of who you are (e.g. sexual orientation or gender identity) can be a stressful and/or liberating experience. Anxiety about who to tell, how, and so on is a common experience for those contemplating coming out. Some ultimately decide not to, and that is okay too. Remember, there is no wrong way or wrong time to come out, and it is always their choice. Here are some practical suggestions for the caller who is considering coming out:

- Plan the encounter. Plan when, where, and the type of environment. Decide ahead of time what will be said, what will not be disclosed and where you will go for support afterwards.
- Choosing a public vs. private place. Depending on the people involved, a private setting may be less embarrassing, or a public setting may prevent an over-emotional or violent reaction.
- It may be best to wait if there are other recent stresses such as a divorce or death in the family. Timing is everything.

- Expect questions from the person you tell. Anticipate them and prepare answers you are comfortable with.
- Give honest answers to questions.
- Weigh the pros and cons of coming out to a particular person(s).
- Do not feel pressure to give details about your sexual activity, who you are currently dating, or anything else you do not wish to disclose.
- Be prepared for any reaction: acceptance, confusion, anger, sadness. This can be the most stressful part of planning to come out: not knowing how the other person will react.
- Have patience with the person you are telling. It may take time for the person to accept this information or even to be able to talk about it with you.
- Have support for yourself afterwards. Plan to meet with a close friend to discuss how it went and to give yourself a sense of security, belonging, and acceptance, especially if the coming out encounter did not go well.
- Most importantly, remember that any negative reactions from others are not about you and are not your fault. Those reactions are about them.

Taking the sex and sexuality call:

Get the caller's **name and age** and allow the caller to take the lead with a **warm opening**.

> *"What's going on tonight?"*
> *"What can I help you with?"*

Develop a **rapport** and gain their *trust* by being **empathic and non-judgmental**. Sex and sexuality calls are fraught with shame issues, and callers will be hyper vigilant to any hint of judgment on our part.

Ask **Open-Ended Questions** to gather the **Big Picture** and determine the caller's needs.

Perception Check to deepen empathy and understand the caller accurately.

> *"So what I hear you saying is that you think you may be gay, but you are not quite sure because you like girls too and that you are feeling very confused about this. Is this accurate?"*

Explore feelings and **Reflect** them back.

> *"I'm hearing a lot of confusion around whether to come out or not."*
> *"You sound like you may be ashamed of these feelings you are having."*
> *"I can hear the frustration when you talk about her."*

Normalize and **Validate** these feelings.

"It's okay to feel angry about this. I would too if I found out my partner had an STD and didn't tell me."

"It's okay to cry. This must be very difficult for you."

"Given what you have been through, I think it is normal that you would feel afraid."

Keep exploring . . .

"When did you first find out?"
"How long have you been exposing yourself?"
"Who else have you told about the abortion?"
"How did they react to you coming out?"
"How has this been affecting your life?"

Summarize the pertinent information back to the caller before moving into problem solving. This is to focus on the core issue and to clarify any misunderstanding so that you will both be on the same page.

"Okay, Jerry, so let me just make sure I've got everything straight before we explore what to do here. You've known that you are gay now for about 5 years and are just now ready to come out to your friends and family. You feel fed up with having to live a lie all the time, but you're scared that people might react negatively to you, and you're not sure what the best way to go about telling them is. Is this right?"

Problem Solving will be about exploring *choices and consequences*. Look at what they would like to have happen first, then discover what they have already tried or thought about to resolve their issue.

"What would be your ideal outcome?"
"What have you thought of doing?"
"What have you tried?"
"How did that work out for you?"
"Who else have you spoken to about this?"

After exhausting all the resources the caller can come up with, then we may offer some of our own **suggestions**. Make sure they are suggestions and not advice.

"Have you thought about seeing a medical doctor about this?"
"Have you considered a support group?"
"Most schools have a LGBTQ organization where you can socialize and talk with others you may feel more comfortable with."

Once you agree upon something, **make a plan** to implement it. Always encourage **small steps** and offer the opportunity for them to call back if they need to.

Resources and Referrals

- For medical concerns, refer to a local hospital, clinic, or health center depending upon cost, insurance, proximity, transportation, etc.
- For psychological and emotional concerns, therapy and support groups can be helpful for expressing feelings in a setting of acceptance.
- Internet sites and social media groups can bring people with common interests or issues together to connect and support each other.
- Planned Parenthood for abortion, STD, pregnancy, or other parenting issues and information.

Toward a Deeper Understanding . . .

SHAME

Guilt is the feeling we experience when we believe we have done something wrong, but shame is felt as "I am wrong" or "I am bad." Shame results from the *belief* that we are somehow lacking and *fundamentally flawed*.

The belief that we are flawed partially stems from our conditioning. More specifically, *expectations* we internalize. Expectations are beliefs about how we *should* be rather than how we are. When we do not measure up to ideals we often feel flawed, less than, inferior, bad, unworthy, unlovable, not good enough.

Much of our shame begins forming in early childhood from repeated experiences with caretakers in which they were not attuned to us and our emotional states, could not tolerate our emotional states, or were not present for us, especially when we were in emotional distress. As we grew, our parents, then our culture, approved or disapproved of us depending on what we did or did not do. The qualities that were judged and disapproved of were often felt to be flawed parts of ourselves, so we repressed them in order to *protect* ourselves from being rejected and abandoned. Unresolved shame often gets passed down from generation to generation.

> *"Toxic shame is experienced as the all-pervasive sense that*
> *I am flawed and defective as a human being . . . It gives you*
> *a sense of worthlessness, a sense of failing and falling*
> *short as a human being." –John Bradshaw*

As shame accumulates, we begin to globalize it to all parts of our being, often leading to depression, mental illness, addictions, violence, and suicide. Our fears of being shamed and hurt again create anxiety and a belief that the world is a dangerous, unfriendly place. Most of the topics covered in this manual are heavily influenced by toxic shame.

The more shame, the more emptiness and disconnection.

The greater the shame, the more we will seek to fill our emptiness with external things we believe can make us feel better (relationships, sex, food, material objects, accomplishments, drugs). Shame motivates both the super-achieving perfectionist and the drug addict.

Shame causes us to wear a mask. We do not like who we are so we pretend to be someone else. We feel insecure and self-conscious. Shame is a relationship killer because it says "don't get too close," crushing intimacy. It may also create an intense neediness, fueled by a yearning to be seen, heard, and cared for in a way that we weren't as a child.

What my shame seeks more than anything is love and acceptance.
The problem is I keep looking to the outside world for this validation. When I do this, I am essentially powerless. I feel unsafe, vigilant that at any moment someone may say or think something bad about me and expose me.
Then I go into protect mode, thinking, I mustn't let my mask down.

In order to experience real lasting love, peace, freedom and connectedness we must heal our shame by bringing it out into the light, little by little.

Healing shame:

"Vision is not enough, it must be combined with venture. It is not enough to stare up the steps; we must step up the stairs." --*Vaclav Havel*

Recommendations for healing shame include working with an empathic therapist you trust and like, practicing mindfulness exercises, reading personal development books about shame (see book recommendation list), and working with your judgments (see Judgment exercises). One of the more powerful and effective therapeutic modalities for working with shame is IFS (Internal Family Systems).

Your old ways and patterns may resist and pull you back in. Just notice and guide yourself back firmly but gently. It takes time and work. Perseverance, patience, empathy, and intention, are the driving forces behind healing shame.

Empathy and Sex and Sexuality

> *"Really good social behavior between people will only*
> *be possible when their awareness is broadened, when*
> *they are able to see the whole situation, to understand*
> *each other more thoroughly, to be aware of each other's*
> *needs and attempt to fulfill that need." –Ramana Mararishi*

Journal on your beliefs about sex. Do you feel sex is something to be ashamed of? Is it dirty? How comfortable are you with your own sexuality?

How comfortable are you talking about sex and sexual matters? Are there specific instances or things you do sexually that you are ashamed of? Explore the underlying beliefs and how you came to believe them.

Notice any feelings of judgment you have toward abortion, different sexual orientations, fetishes, and other sexual matters. Become aware that we are *all equal* in our core worth and *all unique* in how we express ourselves. We have much more in common than we have differences.

Empathize by putting yourself in the shoes of an adolescent who is realizing he is gay and has not told anyone. The school is filled with homophobia. How would you feel? What do you think this person would need?

Journal on any experience you have had with abortion, miscarriage, STDs, sexual dysfunction. How did you feel? How did you cope? What would you have wanted from someone during this time?

EMPATHY DEVELOPMENT

Awareness #3

We are all interconnected.

Everything we think, say, and do affects the whole. Our behaviors ripple outward. Research shows that our thoughts and prayers have effects on others too. When we say or do something hurtful the entire world feels it, especially those closest to us. When we act with kindness, empathy, or loving, the entire planet is raised up. This also means, what I do to others, I do to myself.

> *"The life I touch for good or ill will touch another life,*
> *and that in turn another, until who knows where the trembling stops*
> *or in what far place my touch will be felt."*
> —*Frederick Buechner*

What do you think makes a person want to help another? Why does it feel so intrinsically good to help another? Because we are all connected. My pain is your pain. And your pain is my pain. It is all *our* pain. It is all *our* joy.

If we could visibly see how our thoughts, words, actions, feelings, and most notably our Presence – our energetic field – is affecting everything around us moment to moment – like feedback – we would very quickly begin making new choices.

> *"When one tugs at a single thing in Nature,*
> *he finds it attached to the rest of the world."* –*John Muir*

The more we realize our interconnection with everything and our fundamental Oneness, the more we find ourselves opening up inside and allowing the love that is within to be embodied and ripple outward. Healing our judgments and shame is what creates greater connectedness, because our judgments are the boundaries between us. Boundaries create in-group/out-group thinking, putting limits on our empathic embrace, and creating a pervasive feeling of threat.

> *"Only through our connectedness to others can we really know*
> *and enhance the self. And only through working on the self can*
> *we begin to enhance our connectedness to others."* –*Harriet Goldhor Lerner*

The realization of interconnectedness can significantly expand our empathy and acceptance of others, which allows our hearts to burst open with love and compassion and our bodies to be moved and inspired with the higher purpose of helping others to awaken, grow, and heal.

"Whatever affects one directly, affects all indirectly.
I can never be what I ought to be until you are what you ought to be.
This is the interrelated structure of reality." –Martin Luther King, Jr.

We are all connected *and* we are all separate.
We are the wave *and* the ocean.
In physics, we are the wave *and* the particle.
We are alone *and* we are all One.

ADDICTION

*"Addiction begins by looking for the right thing in
the wrong place."* –Deepak Chopra

Addiction is the compulsive attachment to doing or thinking something that we believe will make us feel better. The high or relief we get is only temporary and as soon as it wears off we go in search of another fix. This attachment can escalate into a physical and/or psychological **dependence**, in which we feel we *need* this fix in order to feel better, be happy, cope, survive, etc. The repeated use of this source builds up a **tolerance**, generating a desire for more of it in order to achieve the same effect.

It soon becomes a habituated coping mechanism, and when we attempt to let it go, stop, or try something different, there are almost always symptoms of **withdrawal**. Whether it is the body left in a state of hyper-arousal or the mind not knowing how to deal with shameful emotions coming to the surface, the uncomfortable and often painful feelings of letting go can often feel too much to cope with. This precipitates us to seek out more of the known source that comforts us, even if it is only temporary.

An addiction becomes a problem when it begins to *negatively affect our life*. As we become totally absorbed in this source of fleeting happiness or relief, other areas of life are neglected, and our body, mind, relationships, finances, and work life can begin to suffer and break down. The more our life breaks down, the more we desire escape from it, and the cycle spins out of control.

We build a love/hate relationship with our addiction. We love the comfort and relief it provides, but resent and hate the power it holds over us as well as the negative consequences of our continued involvement with it.

*"What begins as a search for pleasure soon evolves
into a constant struggle to avoid pain."* –Deepak Chopra

Symptoms of Addiction

- Constantly thinking about the addiction source.
- Needing more and more of it to feel satisfied.
- Neglecting other areas of life.
- Feeling shame, anger, guilt, fear, powerlessness, helplessness.
- Can't control the urge even though it causes huge problems.

<u>Types of addiction</u>

The obvious addictions include drugs, alcohol, smoking, food, and gambling. Lesser known addictions like sex, exercise, shopping/spending, the internet, working, pornography, TV/video games, and caffeine, can also have deleterious effects. We can become addicted to almost anything – another person or even to meditating. Most of these addictions stem from an even deeper addiction – avoidance. Avoidance of pain and uncomfortable feelings.

Why addiction?

> *"Addiction is nothing other than a severely degraded substitute for the true experience of joy."* –Robert Johnson

No one gets through childhood unscathed. Our conditioning inevitably leaves us with wounds and disowned parts that are covered in shame and anxiety. Some of us get larger doses of shame than others, especially those who have experienced trauma, neglect, and/or abuse (physical, emotional, sexual).

Our system didn't have the capacity to handle the pain when it occurred and no one was there to adequately soothe and support us. We then had to adapt and create a strategy (people pleasing, achieving, staying quiet, just to name a few) to help protect ourselves from being hurt again in a similar fashion. The intention was to feel safe, accepted, and in control. These strategies helped us survive our childhoods. But they didn't get rid of the pain.

The unresolved shame and hurt that lurks beneath the surface pushes at the locked basement door, threatening to charge out and overwhelm us the moment we even think of letting down our strategy. Over time, the strategies that helped us to get through tough times creates other problems (pent up anger/resentment, exhaustion, self-sabotage, isolation, physical problems). Cracks begin to form in our defenses. Shame rises, anxiety builds, and helplessness ensues. The needed comfort from our caretakers is still not there, so we turn to the next quickest way to control or turn off this discomfort and incoming pain – alcohol, drugs, sex, video games, food, etc.

But the effects of these external sources don't last. They are fleeting and temporary. The exiled child part within, filled with shame, continues to knock on the basement door, wanting to come up, be seen, heard, held, and comforted. Every time we push them away we add to its pain and shame.

> *"You cannot run away from your problems. Whether it is escape in a liquor bottle or vacationing in exotic lands or finding a new partner. Problems are internal."* –Wayne Dyer

The addictive behavior is an action that actually gives us a feeling of *empowerment,* of regaining control of one's emotional experience and one's life,[15] thus countering the overwhelming feelings of helplessness that arise. The behavior or thought that we choose to overcome this helplessness can become so reinforcing that we do it over and over until it becomes ingrained in us as a mental and physiological pattern. Although we are unconscious of this, it becomes our primary coping mechanism in dealing with and suppressing our pain. Soon, the great feelings of the high will make our present reality feel even lower. We will then need even more of this external source to escape and avoid and comfort.

Every addiction will eventually run itself to excess. A physiological and psychological tolerance is built up and thus it takes more and more to escape and feel good. That excess leads to imbalances in our system. Other areas of life begin to be neglected, like our health, our finances, our relationships, our job, etc. Those breakdowns cause us to feel even more pain, guilt, shame, and anger, and thus we need even more to escape.

We begin to feel more and more out of control, feeling like the source is consuming us. Resentment and anger arise easily and often because this source seems to have so much power over us. A conflict between the desire to let go and the desire to seek more exacerbates our misery and anger.

> *"Love is the most powerful medicine. For love slowly transforms you into what the psychedelics only let you glimpse."* –Ram Dass

Forcing ourselves to stop rarely lasts because we have not dealt with the root of the problem. There is a wounded child part locked away within us, crying out, louder and louder. And it is up to us to take responsibility, turn inward, and help comfort this shamed and scared part of our self.

The love and acceptance we seek are within us. Our core goodness lies beneath and beyond the shame. And when we discover and connect with our core, the energy and truth from it provides the compassion and healing we have sought for so long. The conditioned erroneous beliefs about ourselves then begin to unravel, the shame slowly dissolves, and our need to escape our self relaxes.

Taking the addiction call:

> *"Addiction is the only prison where the locks are on the inside."* - unknown

Each call involving addiction is unique and should be treated as such, however, there are common threads and specific questions to be asked. And do not forget about the Basics – especially dealing with the feelings of the caller.

For a call involving drugs or alcohol:

Check Safety First

Whether the individual is calling to find out information about drugs, or is calling because they have taken drugs, each of these calls require a special sensitivity toward assessing the safety of the individual. This means that we should try to ensure that the caller has not taken dangerous or lethal amounts of a substance and/or they are in a physical environment that is conducive to their personal health and safety.[5]

> *"Where are you?"*
> *"Do you feel safe?"*
> *"Is there anyone else there with you?"*
> *"Have you taken anything tonight?"*
> *"How many?"*
> *"What else?"*
> *"How long ago did you take____?"*
> *"How are you feeling right now?"*

Do not give information on drugs or their effects if you do not know, and do not give advice on how to use them. Instead, ask the caller about *their* usage and/or refer them to an agency that can provide the proper information.

If the call involves an overdose:

- **Gather information in order to send help.**

  > *"What is your address?"*
  > *"What is your phone number?"*
  > *"What is your full name?"*

- **Keep them on the line until help arrives.**

- Let them know that help is on the way.

- If the person is losing consciousness, get them to remain in an upright position, preferably sitting, not standing, otherwise they may fall over and seriously injure themselves. *Shout their name to get them to stay awake and alert as long as you can.*

- If they have lost consciousness, have someone place them on their side, with the head turned toward the floor so that any vomiting will not obstruct the air passages. If no one else is present, continue **getting immediate medical attention** and keep shouting their name.

If the call involves a "bad trip":

The best thing to do is to ensure their safety. This means get them to an area where they feel comfortable and secure. Ask if there is anyone there who is not in an altered state and can offer reassurance. The first goal is to ensure safety (both physical and psychological) and then to get the individual to let go of the fear and experience the trip as positive.[5]

If the call involves an eating disorder like anorexia or bulimia:

Check the seriousness of the disorder by asking open-ended questions about their **symptoms.** Eating disorders can become life-threatening. (Review the end of this section for more information on eating disorders).

> *"How are you feeling?"*
> *"Tell me about your eating habits."*
> *"What do you eat?"*
> *"How often?"*
> *"Do you purge afterward?" "Do you throw it up afterward?"*
> *"Do you use laxatives?"*
> *"How long have you been doing this for?"*
> *"When was your last period?"*
> *"Do you have any hair falling out?"*
> *"How much do you weigh?"*
> *"How tall are you?"*

- Inform them non-judgmentally of some possible consequences of their eating habits.
- Ask if they feel pressured to be perfect. By whom?
- Let them know that it is okay not to be perfect.
- How is their current home/family life? Ask about all their relationships.
- Never say *must* or *should*. This implies pressure and expectations, which their eating disorder is already heavily influenced by.
- It may also be necessary to encourage the caller to eat something, if their health is in jeopardy.
- Inquire about past, present, and future medical attention.
- Refer them to a medical doctor and an eating disorder specialist.

With all addiction calls:

Make sure to do **Perception Checking** throughout:

> *"What I hear you saying is that you have been using cocaine for about three years now and you haven't been able to stop, although you want to. You feel frustrated and angry with yourself because its affecting most*

of your relationships and even your job. And what I really hear you saying is that you want to feel free of this addiction and find some more purpose in your life. Does this sound right?"

Normalize and Validate their feelings in a space of empathy and acceptance.

"Wanting to escape pain is normal. We all have different ways of escaping. Different addictions."

Reflect back feelings while gathering the **Big Picture**.

*"You sound really **frustrated**."*
*"I can hear how **painful** this must be for you."*
*"How has all this work been **affecting you**?" "Your life?"*
*"How does your **family/friends** feel about your gambling?"*
*"**How long** have these shopping sprees been going on for?"*
*"Was there anything that **triggered** you to start doing heroin?"*

Explore more of their **history with the addiction.**

"When is it the worst for you?"
"How do you feel after?"
"How do you feel when you are not doing it?"
"What do you want to do about this?"
"What have you tried to do to stop?"
"Have you sought help before?"
"How did that work for you?"
"What else?"
"What do you think it would take for you to stop?"
"What has this addiction given to you?"
"What has this addiction cost you?"

Explore choices and the consequences of each choice. This will help them to think long-term instead of the usual, impulsive, quick-fix way.

Be careful of your own quick-fix thinking. Do not rush to answers. The exploration and expression of feelings in a space of acceptance is the most important task.

Always explore feelings before problem solving!!

Encourage self-responsibility for their situation (not blame) as the only way to make lasting changes.

"Do you want to stop?"
"What do you think you can do to make a change?"
"How would you like to feel?"
"Are you willing to make a change?"

"What do you think your biggest hurdles are?"

Normalize any fear of change and encourage small steps.

> *"I know change can be scary and it seems like a huge ladder to climb, but without change you will always feel this way and most likely worse. Just take it one small step at a time. We're here to help you do that."*

> *"There are many other people who have and are going through similar circumstances. With help, many people learn to let go and find some happiness."*

Many callers will use the word "*I can't*" to voice their helplessness. Be patient and **help them to see they are already taking empowered action against this helplessness.** Their addiction *is a movement* to help overcome suffering. <u>This action just has to be focused in a healthier direction.</u>

Invite the caller to **take responsibility** for their current situation, and set the intention to take action steps on new choices.

<u>**Make a contract**</u> with the caller, having them commit to a plan of action. Encourage them to take it one small step at a time so as to not overwhelm anyone.

> *Listener:* *"So tomorrow your one step is to seek out and find an AA meeting in your vicinity. Do you agree to do this?"*

Co-Dependency

People who are co-dependents are addicted to relationships with addicts. They focus on helping other people with their problems so that they will not have to face and deal with their own.[16] The hidden belief is that if I help you with your problems and give you lots of nurturing and understanding, then you will love and appreciate me and never abandon me. This leads to a feeling of resentment and of being trapped. We feel afraid to leave the relationship because we feel dependent on the other person to meet our needs.

Resources and Referrals

> ***"Alcohol in Latin is "spiritus," the same word for the highest religious experience as well as for the most depraving poison." –Carl Jung***

<u>*Admitting that we have a problem.*</u>

The biggest step in breaking an addiction is to first admit that we are addicted. Being out of control or addicted to anything is considered *weak* or *bad* in this culture, even though there are very few people who are not addicted to something.

Admitting to an addiction can shake up our sense of identity as a good or strong person, and we will often attempt to rationalize or deny our behaviors.

We may overestimate our power of self-control and underestimate the strength of our dependency.

As listeners, it is not our place to force callers out of denial or dispute their rationalizations. It is also unwise to label them as addicts or diagnose them as an alcoholic, drug addict or anorexic, etc.

For people who admit to having a problem, you job is one of **encouragement:**

- To continue seeking help.
- To learn about their addiction and themselves.
- To be compassionate toward oneself if one falls back into the addictive pattern.
- To be firm and gentle in getting oneself back on course.

"What the undeveloped man seeks is outside. What the advanced man seeks is within himself." –Confucius

AA and Self Help organizations

Alcoholics Anonymous and its offshoot organizations have been estimated to affect, in one way or another, the lives of about 50% of Americans at this time. AA requires no dues or fees. It has no ceremonies, officers or laws, and it owns no property. All AA groups are autonomous and self-supporting. Their 12 steps are only suggestions. They are based around honesty, responsibility, humility and service, practice of tolerance, goodwill and brotherhood.[17] AA and similar approaches have shown to be very effective support in breaking addictions. They help you learn how the drug worked in your life, to learn to avoid using again, get help from others, and work on some inner qualities that can keep you from returning to your old ways.

Offshoot organizations to AA include groups for Narcotics, Cocaine, Overeaters, Sex, Gamblers, Nicotine, just to name a few.

There are groups to support friends and family members of addicted individuals. Nar-Anon and Al-Anon are two such organizations. They can help family members with emotional support and with becoming aware of the ways they may be *enabling* the individual to keep the addiction going.

Rehabilitation and Detox Clinics

Rehab and Detox are especially effective for people who are physically addicted to substances or need to be separated from their environment for their own safety. This gives people time to get the toxins out of their body, understand why they are using these substances, and come up with strategies to deal with possible relapses when they leave the clinic. Detox is a short-term program focused on ridding the toxins from the body, while rehab programs tend to run longer and deal with psychological and behavioral factors.

Changes in environment
Everything in your environment is usually associated with the old pattern. When you are trying to break an addiction, sometimes changes in residence, relationships, and other frequently visited environments can help to keep you from relapsing.

Know Yourself: Therapy and Counseling
Therapy or counseling can help individuals work through emotions, change belief patterns, heal shame, and take further action toward changing one's life. Effective therapy moves the individual from searching in the outer world to discovering and healing in the inner world.

Know Yourself: Reading Books
Reading addiction and self-discovery books can aid immensely in shedding light on the deeper roots for your behaviors, as well as providing practical steps on how to let go and develop empathy and acceptance for yourself.

Know Yourself: Journaling
Journaling helps people organize their thoughts and put their emotions into words. Just 15 minutes a day has shown to increase health and happiness.

Toward a Deeper Understanding . . .

Self-Responsibility

> *"To accuse others for one's misfortunes is a sign of want of education. To accuse oneself shows that one's education has begun. To accuse neither oneself nor others shows one's education is complete." –Epictetus*

To take responsibility for our own actions, words, and feelings is the road to freedom. It is also the road to health and happiness. It does not mean blame yourself. It means realizing, *"I have been doing the best I can, and now that I am aware that I am responsible for how I experience this world, I can take some steps to making some positive changes."*

There are certainly reasons why we feel and act the way we do, such as negative conditioning and traumatic events, but if we keep making excuses or blame others for our current behavior and feelings we will remain stuck, trapped, helpless, powerless.

> *"No one can make you feel bad about yourself without*
> *your permission."* *–Eleanor Roosevelt*

Blame is normal and natural, but it also keeps us shackled in reactivity to the past. In order to break free from the cycle of shame and avoidance, we must access a deeper voice within ourselves. A voice that is wise, compassionate, accepting, and always knows what is best for us. Once we connect with this source of inner guidance, we then have to muster up the willingness and courage to act on it.

Encouraging callers to find this wise inner voice can result in very positive outcomes.

Empathy and Addiction

> *"We see that we can remain calm and choose which thought*
> *we wish to attend to. And we can remain aware behind all these*
> *thoughts, in a state that offers an entirely new level of openness*
> *and insight."* *–Ram Dass*

Journal on identifying some of your own addictions. In what ways do you attempt to escape negative feelings? What are some of the feelings that emerge from your addictions? Do you try to stop your addictions? Describe your inner dialogue? How have your attempts worked for you? How do these addictions affect your life? How do they affect others in your life? If you didn't have these addictions, what would your life experience be like? If you didn't have your addiction, what are you most afraid would happen to you?

Notice your urges and cravings throughout the day. Really feel them. Do not deny them or try to push them away, nor do you have to act upon them. Just be with them. <u>Know that you have a choice in how you respond to these cravings</u>. Ask yourself, what am I really looking for? And can this really be procured with the thing I am craving? Notice if there is a deeper urge to avoid pain or emotional discomfort. Remember, we all have addictions and there is nothing to be ashamed about. It is only through empathy and acceptance that we can move forward.

Be aware that we all want to experience love, peace, freedom, and joy, and we all suffer in trying to attain these. Empathize with this part of yourself that yearns to be free and connected, and just hold this yearning with as much love and compassion as you can without trying to do anything with it.

Empathize with the caller's feelings of helplessness and powerlessness, but also help them to see that they are not as powerless and helpless as they think they are.

<u>**Notice**</u> any feelings of frustration or disappointment that arise in you when a caller resists change or falls back into old patterns. Know that you too have resisted change and have fallen back into old patterns many times. See them as human rather than weak. Judgment and condemnation simply adds shame to their sense of self, which is the main source and perpetuator of the addiction.

Coping with Cravings Practice

When you notice a habitual craving coming on:

1. Pause.
2. Locate the sensations of the craving in your body and bring mindful curiosity to these sensations. Notice them without trying to get rid of them.
3. Count to 90 as you do this.

This will allow the emotional energy and the physiological craving to pass through and dissipate unhindered, which generally takes about 90 seconds. If we fight against the craving or create a story about it or ourselves, it can re-circulate the feelings and even make it stronger.

Drug Information

Stimulants

Also called "uppers," these drugs speed up the central nervous system, decrease appetite, and make a person feel more awake, alert and energetic. Common stimulants include caffeine, nicotine, amphetamines, speed, crystal meth, and cocaine.

Hallucinogens

These drugs alter and distort time, space, and mood, generally producing feelings of unreality. Each person experiences their high differently, and the high is also different each time the individual takes the drug. Common hallucinogens are LSD, ayahuasca, mushrooms, and acid.

Depressants

Also called "downers," these drugs slow down the central nervous system, dampening our natural responses and promoting general feelings of well-being, sleepiness, and relaxation. The individual's motor skills are impaired and their inhibitions reduced. This can lead to sexual acting out or aggression. Alcohol is the most common and most abused depressant. Other depressants include barbiturates, minor tranquilizers (mostly prescription), and narcotics.

Marijuana

Marijuana comes from the Cannabis plant and contains the mind-altering chemical THC. Its effects range from altered senses, changes in mood, impaired body movement, difficulty with problem solving and memory, and in high doses hallucinations, delusions, and psychosis.

MDMA

Chemically similar to both stimulants and hallucinogens, forms of this drug are also known as Ecstasy and Molly. It is a synthetic drug that produces effects such as increased energy, pleasure, emotional warmth, and altered perception. The effects tend to last about three to six hours.

Prescription Drugs

Anti-Depressants

Be aware that the first few weeks of sampling an anti-depressant medication are often among the riskiest in terms of suicide potential. It can increase the person's energy level before any changes in cognition and outlook take effect. Thus, the person is more active but still hopeless and helpless.

SSRI's or Selective Serotonin Reuptake Inhibitors such as Prozac, Luvox, Paxil, Zoloft, and Celexa are the most common anti-depressants. Besides being used for depression, they are also prescribed for bulimia, OCD, panic disorders, PSTD, and others. They take 4-6 weeks to reach maximum effectiveness.

Anti-Anxiety Medication

These medications are used to reduce anxiety and decrease hyper-arousal of the central nervous system. Xanax and Valium are two of the most common ones. They are highly addictive and have abrupt withdrawal symptoms with severe side effects (mania, tremors, vomiting, convulsions, even death). Avoid alcohol when using this medication.

Eating Disorders

> *"Most eating disorders are, initially, efforts to meet a standard of appearance that someone believes will bring happiness. Ultimately, they destroy their bodies trying to make them perfect in the eyes of others."* –Wayne Dyer

Anorexia Nervosa is characterized by an intense fear of gaining weight, self-starvation, body dissatisfaction, distorted perception of body shape or size, and a body weight that is at least 15% below normal.

Some *symptoms and signs* include unusual eating habits and rituals, obsessive or compulsive exercise, isolation from friends and family, and avoidance of social situations where they might have to eat in front of others.

Some *physical effects* include ceased menstrual cycles, hair loss, cardiac problems, low blood pressure, mood swings, changes in metabolism and energy, malfunctioning of pancreas, damaged kidneys and osteoporosis.

Bulimia Nervosa is characterized by bingeing (consuming large amounts of food at one sitting while feeling out of control), purging (getting rid of food by using laxatives, vomiting, obsessive exercise), **intense feelings of guilt and shame**, dissatisfaction with body, and fear of gaining weight.

Some *symptoms and signs* include fear of being fat, eating in secret, hoarding food, mood swings, over-exercising, going to the bathroom immediately following meals, and isolation from friends and family.

Some *physical symptoms* include damaged teeth and swollen cheeks, dehydration, weakness and fatigue, electrolyte imbalance, bleeding and infection of the throat, digestive and intestinal problems, muscle spasms and headaches, irregular menstrual cycles.

Triggers of anorexia and bulimia include low self-worth, family problems, perfectionism, child abuse or rape, as well as cultural beliefs in valuing people based on narrow definitions of physical beauty.

EMPATHY DEVELOPMENT

Releasing Judgments
Exercise #3

Step 1 is to become aware of what our judgments are.
Step 2 is to become aware of why we judge.
Step 3 is to reinterpret our judgments.

By now we are familiar with some of our judgments and why we have them. Now, the next step is to **reinterpret** these qualities and consciously integrate them back into our life. This process will result in greater empathy and life energy, as well as less judgment and reactivity (anger and fear).

Take your five judgment qualities and list them again below:

1.
2.
3.
4.
5.

Reinterpreting qualities simply means looking at them in a different light – from a wider and higher perspective – with more truth. We have labeled these qualities as bad or evil or negative and repressed them into our shadow because we didn't understand their purpose. We feared their expression based on the judgments of others.

Here is an example of the Reinterpretation process:

Judgment Quality: *Aggressive/ Bullying*

Opposite Quality: *Passive*

What would aggression expressed to the extreme look like *to you*?

I am impatient, needy, forceful, bullying, intense, violent, pushy, angry. I create by destroying. I am about action. I go after what I want and nothing is going to stop me. I am tough, strong, attacking, and will fight for what I want, often ruthlessly.

What would passivity expressed to the extreme look like *to you*?

I am lazy, apathetic, weak, wishy-washy, fearful, overly cautious, spineless, and timid. I take very little action, I tend to over think things, have trouble speaking up, and I am easily influenced and susceptible to dogma. I am a pushover. I wait for things to come to me and have no motivation to go after my dreams.

What would a person who was **balanced** with equal parts aggression and passivity look like *to you*?

I am assertive yet calm and patient. I can take consistent action toward achieving goals, yet I also take time to rest and rejuvenate. I stand up for what I want while taking into consideration my deepest values and the effect I have on others. I am open to new information and guidance from my Higher Self and then discern for myself if it works for me by taking action on it. I plan my actions and implement them with perseverance and respect for others.

Describe what it would look like if aggression was channeled in a healthy way?

Assertive. Taking action in service to the highest good. Actively learning. Creating. Participating. Standing up for myself. Setting appropriate boundaries. Being able to say no. Sharing an opinion. Persevering. Evolving. Becoming.

Describe what it would look like if passivity was channeled in a healthy way?

Calm. Relaxed. Patient. Being polite and respectful. Open and receiving what arises in the moment. Spontaneous. Allowing everything to be as it is. Taking time to rest and rejuvenate. Letting things go. Walking away from unnecessary conflicts. Embracing. Being.

If you (aggression part) didn't do your job, what are you afraid would happen?
You would be walked all over, submitting to the will and wants of others, filling up with resentment, feeling powerless, exhausted, and then you would curl up in a ball of depression and shame and emptiness and regret, unable to come out of hiding.

If more aggression was allowed to be expressed, what is your (passive part) biggest concern?
You would end up acting mean and selfishly, hurting others and making people mad at you. You would push them away. They would think you are a bad person and wouldn't want to be around you anymore. You might get in trouble. You will end up alone and ashamed forever.

Integration (aggression)

Three specific ways I can integrate this new energy into my life are:

- ❖ Plan one step of action I can do every day toward a project or goal and do it.
- ❖ Say no to something I don't want at least 2x this week.
- ❖ Call someone I've been waiting to connect with (business or personal).

Now try it for yourself!! Be open, be truthful, be creative! Journaling helps.

Reinterpret one quality at a time. You will feel the results.

Choose a judgment quality from your list.

Judgment Quality_____

Opposite Quality _____

Out of Balance (excess) Judgment Quality
Describe what your judgment quality would look like if it were acted out to the extreme.

_____

_____

_____

_____

Out of Balance (excess) Opposite Quality
Describe what your *opposite* quality would look like if acted out to the extreme.

_____

_____

_____

_____

Integrated (balanced) Qualities
Describe what you think a person would be like if they were perfectly balanced with both qualities.

_____

_____

_____

_____

Describe what your *judgment quality* would look like if it was channeled in a more healthy way?

_____

_____

Describe what your *opposite quality* would look like if it was channeled in a more healthy way?

_____

_____

If you (judgment part) didn't do your job, what are you afraid would happen?

_____

_____

_____

If more (judgment quality) was allowed to be expressed, what is your (opposite part) biggest concern?

_____

_____

_____

Three specific ways I can integrate this new energy into my life are:
(Only make commitments you are going to keep, no matter how small.)

_____

_____

_____

Owning and embodying this new energy or quality may feel a bit uncomfortable at first. Remember, we have been afraid of this quality, this potential, for a long time. We fear what people will think of us *and* it is unknown. When we truly begin to embody this quality, our judgments of it in others will disappear, and in its place – empathy. This doesn't mean we will like this quality being expressed in extreme forms by others, but we will not be triggered by it.

This judgment work may seem like a waste of time to some people, but it is absolutely necessary if we want to grow, heal, deepen our empathy, and become powerful facilitators of positive change in the world.

Here are some recommendations when doing this work:

Be Patient with yourself, and keep practicing. These changes do not usually happen over night. It takes Perseverance, Commitment, Honesty, Willingness, and Openness. The more difficult we find the reinterpretation to be, the deeper and more ingrained the judgment. Keep looking deeper. Keep working with it. Work with a therapist on the roots of the judgment. There is probably an amazing gift of creative energy waiting for you.

Work on one judgment at a time. You are bringing light to those darkened, shamed aspects within yourself little by little. Too much light too quickly and we tend to back away and resist.

Be gentle with yourself. This is a process. A human learning process. Do not judge yourself for judging. Be compassionate and kind with yourself on this journey. Self-punishment is what you are leaving behind.

CRISIS

What is crisis?

A crisis is defined as an <u>acute emotional upset</u> triggered by an event or situation that is *perceived* as intolerable and temporarily exceeds a person's resources and coping mechanisms. A person is not only upset about the crisis situation itself but also upset by their inability to cope.[3]

In the midst of a crisis, we cannot make sense of what is happening or why it is happening. Without answers to these important questions, we are left feeling **helpless**. We simply do not know what to do to control or master the situation. We do not know how to make it stop. Wave after wave of emotion sweeps over us and we are unable to predict when or if this awful situation is going to end.[18]

A Crisis always involves a loss, whether it is real or threatened, that satisfies a vital psychological need.[19] The loss could be the death of a loved one, a job, health, financial security, control, identity, trust or safety, material possession, feeling of self-worth, or a hope or dream. Generally, the more unanticipated the loss, and the greater the loss or perceived loss is to our survival and safety, the greater the chance for crisis – as in cases of abuse, rape, and sudden deaths.

When the loss is deemed to be beyond our coping abilities, denial becomes the initial defense, shutting down and repressing any emotions and thoughts about the event. But any reminder of the loss or any new stressor will cause those denied emotions and thoughts to bubble up and squeeze through the cracks, engaging the defenses to work even harder, using up more energy. The more life energy we use up defending, the more we create a world of fear and perceived threat and danger. If the feelings and thoughts are not dealt with, eventually our abilities to function in the world could spiral downward to the point of mental illness.

The <u>perception</u> of events is the major cause of the crisis. It has little to nothing to do with the thing or loss itself. <u>Something that is a crisis for one person may not be a crisis for another</u>. Our individual **beliefs** about ourselves and the world are the roots of what forms our perceptions. And if we perceive that we are losing something that we desperately need in order to survive or be happy, we may end up in a state of crisis.

> ***"You cannot solve a problem from the same level of consciousness that created it."*** *–Albert Einstein*

In Chinese, the character for <u>crisis means both danger and opportunity.</u> Growth is always preceded by a state of imbalance or crisis. Insight and a change of perception can lead to a higher level of functioning than was present before the crisis began. During a crisis a person is often more receptive to help and change. Crises are a part of life and should not be considered abnormal.

The second factor in crisis is our window of tolerance. This window refers to the degree to which our nervous system can handle, cope, and regulate the emotions and physiological sensations being experienced in the moment. If the feelings exceed our window, then our system may end up closing down into a freeze response (disconnection, dissociation) or flying open into fight/flight response which may in turn generate a panic attack, rage, extreme impulsivity, emotional outburst, or obsessive and compulsive thoughts/behaviors. The Tools and Resources for Dealing with Anxious Callers section listed earlier in the book can be helpful for callers outside their window of tolerance.

P.T.S.D. (Post Traumatic Stress Disorder)

PTSD applies to people who have been severely traumatized at one or more times in their lives and at present are not functioning effectively because they have not integrated the trauma. This disorder is most prevalent in war veterans, survivors of child abuse and rape, battered women, and victims of violent crimes. It is also seen in witnesses to murders or deaths, and people who live through natural disasters and car accidents.[20]

Initially, there is a shock phase that allows the person to cope with overwhelming emotions. Then as the reality seeps in, the emotions burst forth. Common symptoms include: *depression, hypervigilance, intense fear and helplessness, nightmares, reliving the experiences in one's mind over and over, and difficulty in relationships.* Their sense of **safety in the world has been shaken,** and they spend a vast amount of their energy defending against fearful emotions.

These feelings cannot be denied forever. They must eventually be dealt with and integrated in order to move back to a healthy level of functioning. Once the individual has allowed the trauma to surface, a flood of feelings will be aroused. Professional help is then needed to process the trauma, complete defensive responses (fight or flight), alter limiting beliefs formed from the trauma ("it was my fault, I'm bad"), and channel feelings into productive avenues of growth by finding some new, higher meaning in the event.[20]

Taking the crisis call:

"For the person who is faced with a crisis, the very sound
of a caring, thoughtful voice can provide emotional support,
analogous to the giving of a blood transfusion to the physically
wounded." –David Lester

Crisis intervention is a short-term helping process focusing on the immediate problem through the use of personal, social, and environmental resources.

There are many different levels of crisis. **A very urgent crisis** will require an immediate response within minutes – ambulance, medical attention, police, crisis outreach. Get the person's name, address, and phone number in order to send help, or give them an appropriate referral as soon as possible. We may have to get them out of the house or out of danger first. Keep them on the phone as long as you can unless it is impeding their **safety** in that moment.

Many of the following sections involve **urgent crisis** calls such as rape, abuse, domestic violence, and suicide. Sometimes people become so overwhelmed they contemplate escape by suicide. If we receive any hint of suicide, do not hesitate to ask (see suicide section).

The **less urgent crisis** involves callers who are likely to be very upset and disoriented. They cannot make sense of or understand what has happened. They ask questions such as *"Why did this happen?" "Why me?" "It just doesn't make any sense!" "What did I do?"* The caller complains of not knowing what to do and expresses a loss of ability. We hear their sense of helplessness and feel a very strong pull to intervene actively and take control of the situation.

If the level of upset is so great that the caller cannot even talk or is incoherent (outside their window of tolerance), help them to calm down first with either a simple **breathing exercise** or one of the other tools in the The Tools and Resources for Dealing with Anxious Callers section.

> *"I can hear that you are very upset right now. That's okay. I'm here*
> *to help you. But first I need you to take a couple of deep breaths*
> *with me. Breathe in very slowly . . . now let the air all the way out. Good.*
> *Let's try that again."*

Your voice should be slow, calm, and gently reassuring but unmistakably in control. As listeners, we may have to be more active than normal, providing organization for the caller in crisis, and **breaking the story up into smaller manageable portions**.

> *"How did it start?"*
> *"What happened next?"*
> *"What did you do?"*
> *"How do you feel about that?"*

Encourage the expression of feelings, but if the emotions become too intense and overwhelming for the caller, help them to just *describe* the events that have taken place without emphasizing the feelings. There will be opportunity to come back to feelings later.[5]

A general crisis call involves:

- Empathizing.
- Perception Checking and Reflecting Feelings.

- Gathering the Big Picture.
- Problem solving and developing a plan.
- Implementing the plan and drawing on resources available to the caller.

Gather the **Big Picture** by assessing the individual's *current emotional state*, the trigger events, their perceptions of those events, and their current level of functioning and coping.

> **Reflecting** feelings back to a caller helps them gain insight into how they are coming across to you. This lets them step outside of themselves for a moment, which often diffuses the intensity of their emotions. Meet their intensity level as best as you can, as calmly as you can, keeping your intensity level just below or just above theirs, depending if they sound too activated or too down.

> > *"There is a part of you that is really overwhelmed right now, huh?"*
> > *"I can sense that you are quite angry about this."*
> > *"You sound really down. It seems like a part of you feels hopeless, huh?"*

> Be **Empathic** as you **Normalize and Validate** their feelings.

> > *"It's perfectly normal to be scared after losing that much money."*

> > *"It's okay to be angry. I might be too if I thought I was fired for something I didn't do."*

> > *"This must be really hard for you. It's understandable that you would feel this way."*

> > *"It sounds like a lot of things have been happening all at once, any one of which you could handle, but together I can see how you would be overwhelmed by them."*

> Ask **Open-Ended questions** to find out what the trigger event (loss) was.

> > *"Did something happen?"*
> > *"Tell me what you are scared about?"*
> > *"What do you think is going to happen?"*

> Explore their **perceptions and meanings** of the trigger events. Everyone sees things differently. A failed test might not mean anything to one person and might be the end of a dream for another.

> > *"It sounds like this job meant a lot to you and that you feel you will not be able to find another one that pays the money you need to survive."*

> > *"You're saying that you can't picture living without this person in your life?"*

> *"I hear you saying that you believe you are a failure because you didn't get into law school. Is that accurate?"*

Notice your judgments! Remember the reality of the caller is the reality of the call. Just because something is not important to you, does not mean it is not for someone else. If you feel triggered by something they say, notice your feelings, internally ask that part of you to step back, then re-engage your curiosity to understand the caller's point of view.

Assess the person's coping skills, level of functioning, and support. Ask about the effects this is having on their relationships, as well as their work and school lives.

> *"How have you been dealing with this so far?"*
> *"How is this affecting your life right now?"*
> *"Is there anyone you feel you can talk to about this?"*
> *"How do you usually deal with stressful situations?"*

People in crisis often feel overwhelmed, and they may overwhelm *you* by presenting a shopping list of problems to be solved. You will need to **break down the problem into manageable pieces** and work them through one at a time.[19]

> *"It sounds like you are going through a lot right now. Let's see if we can work on one thing at a time. What is most important to you?"*
>
> *"You seem most concerned about your car, so let's begin with that."*

Once the problem is defined and their feelings and perceptions are explored, then you can work on **problem solving.** Explore what they *have* tried and what they *would like to* try, then brainstorm other alternatives and offer suggestions.

> *"What have you tried?"*
> *"What would you like to try?"*
> *"What else can you think of to try to get through this?"*
> *"What would you tell a friend to do in this case?"*
> *"What helps you to feel better, more in control?"*
> *"Have you ever talked to a counselor or therapist?"*
> *"How would you feel about going to a support group?"*

Make concrete plans with them in a step-by-step fashion and only for the next couple of days. A person in crisis does not absorb a lot of information nor can they foresee too far into the future.

Gently educate the caller as to what they might expect for the next couple of days during the acute phase of the crisis. Let them know that they are likely to experience a roller coaster of feelings and that this emotional upheaval is very normal after experiencing such an upsetting event. Encourage them to call back at any time when things feel like too much for them.

Toward a Deeper Understanding . . .

Beliefs

"We become what we believe about ourselves." *–Unknown*

Our beliefs are the most determining factor in how we think, act, and feel. It is our beliefs that lay out our pattern of responses in life. If you change a belief, you change the entire pattern of your life. The most influential beliefs are the ones we hold about ourselves, the world, and our future.

Traumas often shake up our beliefs, altering them in ways which increase anxiety, helplessness, anger, and shame. We may lose trust in ourselves and the world and then form coping strategies that lead to impulsivity, acting out, and/or isolation and withdrawal.

Our beliefs about who we are – **our identity** – will impact all of our other beliefs. Are we good or bad at our core? Am I gross, disgusting, broken, worthless, unlovable, not enough? Or am I good, have equal core value to others, and am doing the best I can given my circumstances and conditioning? Am I less than, more than, or equal to others?

Generally, people resist changing their beliefs about who they are because changing these beliefs would shake up their entire life. They serve as our control center. When we try to force our behaviors to change without addressing the underlying beliefs, we will face great resistance and our old patterns will eventually pull us back in. When we try to force others to change their core beliefs, we may encounter their resistance. Our history books are replete with struggles and wars having to do with our fundamental beliefs about ourselves, others, and the world.

"Shifting, changing or expanding identity can produce the most profound and rapid improvement in the quality of your life." *–Tony Robbins.*

While our beliefs provide us with a sense of control, they can also be limiting, especially if we hold them too rigidly or they are not true. Changing our limiting beliefs can help us to overcome obstacles to our inner growth and external goals. We must first explore what our inner and outer goals are, then become aware of what beliefs are helping us and what beliefs are hindering us. Next, come up with new more rational, truthful, and empowering beliefs, and then practice substituting them whenever you feel the old limiting beliefs coming up.

MENTAL ILLNESS

Callers who are suffering from Schizophrenia, Bipolar Disorder, Borderline Personality disorder, or Dissociative Identity Disorder (DID) often present issues and crisis that are particularly difficult for listeners to deal with.

People with mental disorders often feel marginalized. They feel they really do not fit into society. Perhaps the most important thing to remember in taking a call from a person with a mental disorder is that the person still has feelings, no matter how flat the affect or garbled the speech, and while we often cannot help guide them to an understanding or resolution of these feelings, *the feeling state must be respected*. The reality of the caller, no matter how distorted or surreal, is still the reality of the call.[5]

Schizophrenia

Psychiatrists and medical researchers have little information about schizophrenia and the factors that cause the disorder. The onset usually occurs in the late teens/early twenties with the first "psychotic break" or the first episode in which the individual suffers from <u>hallucinations, delusions, and possibly catatonia</u>. Most show a decrease in overall functioning and have difficulty taking care of themselves on a basic level. They often require constant, adequate dosages of medication, which many have trouble maintaining due to their lack of self-care skills. In addition, most people with schizophrenia lack the social and academic skills necessary to secure adequate job functioning. It has been known as the homeless disorder.[5]

Their communication may go round and round, or be repetitive, tangential, and disorganized. Sometimes people with schizophrenia may be <u>paranoid or delusional</u>, believing that others are out to harm them. These individuals may believe that their spouse is cheating on them or that someone is poisoning their water. It is not our place to rebuke these fantasies or to buy into them. Saying *"It sounds like you need help to resist these voices"* or *"It sounds like this is triggering a lot of distress for you"* would be more helpful for all.

Bipolar Disorder

Individuals with this disorder tend to go up and down between feelings of <u>mania and depression</u>. The manic phase is characterized by feelings of power, increased energy, little need for sleep, delusions of grandeur, wild or uncharacteristic behavior, and increased drug and alcohol use. As this phase passes, it is typically followed by a period of deep depression and feelings of hopelessness. Many have to be hospitalized and receive treatment. Lithium is the standard medication treatment, working to shrink down the emotional range of the person to a steady modulated state. But many bipolar patients stop taking the Lithium because the high they feel in the manic state is better than any drug. They just want the lows taken away.[5]

Dissociative Identity Disorder

Virtually every known case of this disorder revolves around individuals who have suffered severe abuse, typically physical and/or sexual. Most come to treatment confused because they have blackouts, find strange clothes in the closet, have strangers recognize and greet them as old friends, and often have other social problems. What is most remarkable about this disorder is that the individual has actually created separate personalities – some with different ages and even different sexes.[5]

Borderline Personality Disorder

These individuals tend to have few boundaries, express extreme emotions, have unstable relationships, and can be highly labile (moving back and forth in their emotional states). They often present themselves as depressed, feeling dead or lifeless inside, empty, without energy, goal-less, and highly suicidal. Callers with this disorder can make you feel like you are the only one in the world who can help them, but when they feel that you have chastised them or cannot help, you become the epitome of evil, and they can become verbally abusive.[5]

Taking the Mental Disorder Call

While taking calls with less challenging people, we strive to uncover feelings that are beneath the surface. That is not always the best strategy with severely disturbed people. In general, they are being flooded or overwhelmed by too many feelings and need to find a way to put the lid on the torrent of emotions they are experiencing. If so, do not ask the caller to tell you more about their feelings. Instead use *calming interventions, like breathing exercises and short questions to break their experience into manageable chunks.* Feelings are acknowledged but are not made the main focus of the conversation.

Speak in clear, straightforward terms. Refrain from jokes.

Callers who exhibit dissociative traits are very challenging and are often beyond our scope of help. What we *can* do is listen and continue using our basic skills as with any other call. If the caller switches personalities, stay calm and maintain confidentiality between each personality. Do not attempt to integrate or have the personalities communicate with one another.

Always ask if they are seeing a therapist. If they are not, encourage them to go see one or reconnect with a former one.

Medications

When appropriate, find out about the medications the caller is using. Ask if they have been taking them on the schedule recommended by the physician. If the caller has discontinued use of medications without consulting their physician, encourage the caller to contact the prescribing physician to discuss the management of medication. Also, we may need to inform callers that some medications take a few weeks to begin working and to recommend continued usage until talking to the physician.

CHALLENGING CALLERS

Sometimes we may feel frustrated or angry with callers that block the way for good open communication. Callers who are abusive, manipulative, angry, masturbating, or the classic "yes, butters." To deal with these callers, we can use "I" Messages.

"I" Messages

In the "I" Message, we explain to callers how we feel, why we feel that way, and what they can do to remedy the situation. It takes the form of the following statement:

I feel (emotion) when you (behavior) because (reason).

> *"I feel a little frustrated when you don't consider any of the options we have been talking about because it makes me wonder whether you are really interested in taking action to deal with your problem."*

> *"I feel uncomfortable when you ask me personal questions about myself because I'm here to listen and help you with the things that are bothering you."*

You are talking about their <u>behavior</u> and not them as a person.

<u>Focusing a caller</u>

> A caller may also tell us what seems like a hundred different problems, going without pause from one to the next. Our job is to <u>focus</u> the caller on one **core issue** and explore that.

> *"It sounds like a lot is going on in your life right now. But it seems as if your family is troubling you the most. Why don't we focus in on them first."*

> *"Which of these problems would you like to work on right now?"*

> *"What do you see as the main issue for you today?"*

<u>Focusing on feelings</u>

A caller who focuses on the content only makes it more challenging to move the call to a feeling level. Remaining with the content keeps the call superficial. Our specialty is feelings.

"You have told me a lot about the situation, but I am not going to give my opinion. I would like to hear how this has affected you and what your feelings are."

"What I would really like to focus on are your feelings and how you are coping."

Sometimes you may have to focus a caller away from <u>sexual details</u> and onto feelings.

"I am much more concerned with your feelings surrounding the situation rather than the sexual details. Let's talk about your feelings."

"Yes Butting"

Most callers express some resistance to change. In fact, most people do. However, there are those callers who seem to be stuck in a rigid trough of resistance, almost determined not to take any action toward working out of their misery. They feel like they have tried everything or that they would inevitably fail. Often it is a part of them that is afraid of getting their hopes up and experiencing another painful disappointment. Yet, they keep us on the phone, continuing to discuss the problem asking for help. One part of them wants help and another part won't receive it. This can be extremely frustrating for listeners, who feel shot down time after time by the frequently heard phrase, *"Yes, but—."* Sometimes expressing our own frustration can be beneficial for both us and the caller. However, we must own our own emotions and not put them on the caller by saying, *"You are <u>making</u> me frustrated."*

"You know, when you say 'yes but'. . . to me, I feel a little frustrated. I am trying to help you find a solution, and it seems that every time I say something, you have a reason for why it won't work. If you were to try one of these suggestions, what are you afraid might happen?"

"It seems as though we have been talking about possible solutions to your problem for a while now, and I think we've come up with some pretty good ideas, but none of them seem to resonate with you. Why do you think that is? I'm getting the feeling that you really just want me to fix it or for it to just go away."

This may provide a new experience for the caller. More often than not these people have been confronted with hostile and frustrated people who have shamed and rejected them. Making the frustration our own, and sticking by the caller empathically while confronting the situation, the caller may learn something about how they are in the world.[3]

Be patient and empathic. Remember, we all resist change to some degree. Inform them that they are not as helpless as they think they are. Encourage tiny risks and small steps. They have already taken the first step in calling the crisis line.

Our frustration may also be a sign we are trying to fix, save, rescue, or change them in some way. Be aware of these feelings within and then let them go. Trying to save or fix someone keeps them in a helpless place while seeing them as flawed. They will be open to change only when *they* are ready.

Sexual Gratification Caller

The caller whose sole purpose is to masturbate to your voice is seldom interested in working on or resolving his problem – deriving sexual gratification by making use of an unknown person's voice rather than from a relationship characterized by mutual intimacy. Nevertheless, our job is to remain polite and respectful, and in these situations, firm, appropriate, and consistent in our approach.[3]

Characteristics of sexual gratification callers include:

- Voice devoid of feelings.
- Hesitation in speaking or a great deal of silence.
- Unusual breathing.
- Presents self with boyish innocence about sexual matters.
- Will not speak to a man, but often requests to speak to one.
  "Is there a man I can speak to there?"
- Asks listener's opinions about his sexual problem with insistence.
- Asks listener personal questions.
- Common story themes in presenting problem: Sex with female member of the family, lending his wife/girlfriend to another man, enjoying sex with young boys/girls, being exposed nude against one's will.
- Resistance toward any resolution of the problem. He just keeps repeating his narrative.
- Focuses on specific graphic sexual details.
- Asks for sex information or referrals, but then refuses to take them.

Success with these types of callers, i.e., helping them to see that this behavior is problematic, is very rare. Experienced listeners become quite jaded about these types of callers and new telephone crisis specialists are often unrealistically optimistic about what can be done.[3]

When we think this person may be masturbating, we can:

Focus him on feelings and dealing with his problem and away from details. If he consistently brings the call back to details and does not want to take any action, *politely* tell him, *"Well, I don't think that I can help you tonight."* And then hang up.

When we get a very strong intuition that this caller is masturbating, we confront, giving them the opportunity to talk about this problem. If they refuse, hang up.

"I'm getting the sense that you are masturbating right now. If you want to talk

about why you feel the need to masturbate to people's voices, I'm open to that, otherwise I'm going to end this call."

When confronted, most of these callers will simply hang up. A telephone crisis specialist does not have to feel obliged to be the inappropriate sexual stimuli for this type of caller.

Staying on the line with them serves to enable them and demonstrates to them that there are no consequences for making sex calls. Ending the call stresses that they need to take responsibility for their behavior, and for helping themselves. It shows them that, if they really want to stop, they have to ask directly.[21]

Sexual gratification callers tend to have low self-worth and insight into their behavior. They often feel helpless to stop themselves. Some agencies believe it can be beneficial to help the caller understand that making sex calls is a sign of a problem that they would need outside help for. Showing them that we value them enough to still try to work with them, even after recognizing that they were attempting to exploit us by making a sex call, can have tremendous healing potential and may make it more likely they seek outside support.[21]

It is best if the agency develops a written policy in dealing with sexual gratification callers in order to delineate firm boundaries and empower listeners to deal with these interactions in an assertive manner.

Angry and Abusive Callers

Encountering anger, annoyance, sarcasm, and frustration are inevitable parts of your job as listeners. Do not take it personally. <u>Accept their feelings and reflect back to them to diffuse the intensity.</u>

> *"It sounds like you're feeling angry about something. Did something happen today?"*

It may seem as if a caller is angry or yelling at *you*, but more than likely they are angry about other things. However, it is appropriate to gently confront a caller with an *I Message* if you are becoming uncomfortable with their anger.

> *"I feel uncomfortable when you raise your voice because it makes it difficult to listen and help you with what is bothering you."*

> *"I'm wondering if it would be more helpful for you to call back later when you feel less irritated."*

What if the caller becomes abusive?

"I feel uncomfortable when you call me names and threaten me. I'm going to end the call now."

What if a caller attacks your style of reflective listening?

"You seem irritated by the way I respond to you. I'm just making sure that I understand what's going on and how you are feeling so I can help you better."

We are never, ever, expected or required to remain on the line with an abusive caller. However, if the caller is simply someone we do not like or has an issue that is personally difficult for us, our first commitment is to the caller and we must do our best to deal with these issues without personal interference.

Make sure to set firm limits with callers who are becoming abusive. We are not here to take that. When you say you are going to hang up . . . do it. You are always in control of the call. Give them a chance, but if they continue, hang up. Hanging up on an abusive caller who will not stop is taking care of yourself.

What if a caller wants to know my credentials?

When someone asks questions about our experience and credentials, more often than not what they really want to know is, *"Are you going to be able to understand me?"* and *"Can I trust you?"* Instead of becoming defensive, respond to the caller's need.[3]

"I am a trained (your job title). I think you are wondering if I can understand and help you? Why don't you tell me the problem and we'll see?"

Almost any caller can pick us apart. Do not get caught up in explaining yourself, but turn the conversation with a remark such as:

"I don't think this is what you called to talk about."

Manipulative Callers

A caller who uses manipulation places us in an uncomfortable position by asking us to compromise our role as a listener. They want us to exceed the boundaries of the helping relationship by asking us to take on responsibilities or roles that are not ours. For example, the caller threatens to commit suicide if you attempt to end the call, or the caller insists she needs to tell you the details or she will not be able to talk about her feelings. A caller may even want to meet us outside the line or give information that is against the regulations of the line.

As listeners we may find ourselves getting hooked because the caller sounds so desperate. We fear the caller may take action on their threat. We may even become worried they will not like us if we do not answer their questions or do as they ask.

The most effective approach is to Perception Check and use **Reflection** to focus on their feelings of *desperation* and *helplessness*. Bend over backwards to stay with this approach. Stay calm and do not display your discomfort.

> *"You sound really hurt and offended that I won't get involved."*

Remain objective and curious and do not get hooked by the cry/demand for help. Remember the caller is responsible for their own actions and feelings. Do not let the caller corner you into believing that you should feel sorry for them or that you should take action to change the situation.

> *"It sounds like you desperately want me to do something to change the situation. I can't do that, but I can help you sort out what you'd like to do."*

Maintain boundaries of what the crisis line can do. Be very articulate that we are not in a position to become involved in the situation. Remember, the listener's role is to empower the caller to be responsible for their own behavior. We are not in a position to take away pain.

Confronting

The term confrontation has a frightening stigma attached to it for many people, especially sensitive listeners looking to resolve conflict, not start some. Confronting does not mean getting in someone's face in an angry way. It simply means **focusing on an issue in a direct way, taking control, and letting the caller know your boundaries and what is expected for the call to continue.** It is an assertive, yet non-aggressive, response. Some people find the term *care-frontation* helps them to be assertive while maintaining empathy and compassion.

For example, if a caller is going in circles, asking for help, but reluctant to try anything at the same time, eventually the caller will have to be confronted:

> *"It seems as if you're not ready to take any steps right now toward*
> *making a positive change in your life. If you want to talk about why,*
> *I'm more than willing, but if not, I'm going to open up the line for other*
> *callers and you can call back another time."*

Confronting the caller lets them know that we are not just going to sit back and listen to the same stories of helplessness over and over. Some action must be taken, and eventually the reluctant, resistant caller must be confronted with this.

However, listeners should always remain aware of the temptations to use confrontation to validate one's own sense of power.[7]

When we suspect a caller is masturbating, we confront them:

> *"I'm getting the sense that you are masturbating right now. If this*

is true, I'm going to have to end this call."

When someone is abusive toward us, we confront them:

> *"When you yell at me, I feel uncomfortable because I trying to help you. If you want to talk about what is really bothering you, I'm willing to do that. If not, I'm going to end this call."*

Resources and Referrals

For all medical concerns, we refer callers to a hospital, clinic, or health center. To deal with psychological or emotional issues, we can suggest therapy or counseling, self-help, psychology or spiritual books to learn about the Self, journaling, stress management courses, exercise, nutrition, and meditation. Be creative, there are no limits to what could be helpful for people.

Empathy and Crisis

> **"Responding with empathy, we strengthen our relationships with others and with the world at large, expand our horizons, broaden our perspective, and get the added bonus of feeling good about ourselves."** –*Power of Empathy*

Journal on a time in your life when you were in a crisis – feeling overwhelmed and frightened. What else did you feel? What did you lose and/or what were you scared of losing? How did you cope? What did you do? And how did you alter your view of the situation to come back into balance? What would you have wanted from others in that situation?

Empathize with a person's feelings of **helplessness** in a crisis situation. Know how scary it is to be in that state and how the urge to escape becomes extremely powerful. Relate to the feeling of being *trapped in not knowing what to do,* how to escape, or how to soothe oneself.

Notice any feelings of discomfort you have when listening to a person who is in crisis. Be aware of the feeling of *helplessness* in you. This may lead to an urge to *rescue* this person in need. Just notice these feelings, then choose to stay calm and do the best you can to help this person take positive action toward coping with their crisis. It is part of your job to help them see that they are not helpless in this situation. We act like mirrors, reflecting back to them their inner strength and goodness.

Be aware of any judgments you have toward people who play helpless or do not take the action you want them to take. Notice any judgments you have toward people who are in crisis over something that seems insignificant or trivial to you. Remember, there are probably things you have felt overwhelmed about that others thought were silly.

Contemplate whether the universe is friendly to you or not. Is it supportive or out to get you – or neither? You are encouraged to examine this belief. How did you come to believe this? Anything from the past? Is it really true?

EMPATHY DEVELOPMENT

Awareness #4

At our core, we are all perfect.

Our belief that we are *lacking* something fundamental comes from not knowing who we truly are. And we will often see others through the same lens as we see ourselves. We are not just our qualities or our personality. These are *expressions* of who we are. The essence of who we are is Love and Goodness, and our journey is to become aware of and embody this truth.

When we identify with only our personalities and qualities, we automatically own some qualities and disown others. We will then judge others who express our disowned qualities. A boundary goes up between us and them, we label them as bad, and we experience an "againstness" toward them. In our minds, they become flat and lifeless. There is no common ground in which to relate, in which to empathize, in which to connect.

Imagine how liberating it would be if we were to stop trying to change others and just accept people as they are. And besides, no amount of judging or wishing they were different is going to change the way they are *right now*.

> **"We cannot see anyone as they really are when we are looking through the lens of one of our identities. Then the other is only the extension of the psychology of that particular identity – someone who pleases us or threatens us. But when you see others as simply who they are, then you can regard them with compassion."** *–Richard Moss*

When I look into a person's eyes, I see behind the clouds of pain and defenses and directly into the perfect love and goodness of their core. And I see an *ever-changing* human trying to survive, trying to get free and reach full potential, yearning to love and be loved, seeking to understand and know oneself, struggling with pain and limiting beliefs. Seeing the core perfection in all people, starting with ourselves, is necessary to making a deeper empathic connection with someone.

Let the core perfection and goodness in you *connect* with the core perfection and goodness in another, and you will discover that there really is no "other." No matter what state you or they are in, this perfection is always there. This essence – this love – is ever present.

Knowing the core perfection and potential in ourselves and seeing it in others is a powerful engine for healing and growth.

CHILD ABUSE

Statistics:

- In 2015, approximately 2.2. million of 4 million reports to Child Protective Services (CPS) were deemed "appropriate" for investigation of the safety and well-being of approximately 4.1 million children.[22]
- 90% of abuse victims know their assailant. Half occur in the child's home.[23]
- There are approximately 60 million child sexual abuse survivors in the U.S.[23]
- 1,670 children died in 2015 as a result of child abuse.[22]
- Only about 33% of child sexual assaults are reported.[24]
- Children who have been sexually abused are 2.5 times more likely to abuse alcohol and 3.8 times more likely to become addicted to drugs. [24]
- One third of abused and neglected children will later abuse their own children, continuing the cycle of abuse. [24]
- 325,000 children are at risk of becoming victims of commercial child sexual exploitation each year.[25]

Physical abuse includes any intentional physical injury. It also encompasses **neglect,** which is the failure, refusal, or inability by a parent or guardian to provide necessary food, clothing, shelter, education, supervision, or health care that seriously endangers the child.

Psychological/Emotional Abuse refers to any rejection, intimidation, or humiliation of a child that undermines their sense of self-worth and well-being. It may include withholding love and affection. This type of abuse is characterized by a pattern of negative behavior and not just an isolated incident or two resulting from the normal ups and downs of parental emotions.[19]

Sexual Abuse refers to a child being forced or tricked into sexual activity. This includes everything from obscene phone calls, to fondling, vaginal, oral or anal penetration. Making a child watch sexual movies or pose for seductive or sexual photographs is considered child sexual abuse. Any kind of voyeurism or exhibitionism that is sexually stimulating to a parent, or inappropriate sexual behavior or talk in front of young children can also prove harmful.

Incest is any family member that performs inappropriate sexualized behavior toward a child. A family member is defined as anyone the child perceives to be in the role of a family member.

The long-term effects of child sexual abuse can be so pervasive that it is sometimes hard to pinpoint exactly how the abuse has affected a person. It permeates everything: our sense of self, our intimate relationships, our sexuality, our parenting, our work life, even our sanity.[27]

The way the abuse is handled when we are children has a lot to do with its subsequent impact. If a child's disclosure is met with compassion and effective intervention, the healing begins immediately. But if no one noticed or responded to the child's pain, or if they were blamed, not believed, or suffered future trauma, the damage is compounded.[27]

> ***"The effects of child sexual abuse can be devastating
> but they do not have to be permanent." –****Courage to Heal*

Consequences of Child Abuse

Immediate safety concerns include the pains and wounds of any forced sexual contact, STD's, and pregnancy. Many develop low self-worth, blaming themselves for the abuse. This manifests with self-destructive behaviors and intense urges to escape the painful emotions. The child will often feel *violated, humiliated, dirty, and guilt ridden. Their sense of safety and well-being has been shattered.*

Common signs of children who have been abused:

- Recurrent nightmares and sleep disturbances.
- Withdrawal and turning off feelings.
- Depression and suicidal behavior.
- Eating disorders/ Distorted body image.
- Drug and alcohol addiction.
- Dissociation.
- Masturbates at inappropriate times and places.
- Inappropriate or precocious maturity, including sexual behavior (prostitution).
- School delinquency, underachievement, distraction, daydreaming.
- Seeks approval by trying to be perfect.
- Fear/distrust of authorities.
- Poor peer relationships.
- Patches of hair missing, inexplicable burns and bruises, cutting.

Later on in adulthood the results can be:

- A lack of trust in themselves and others.
- Trouble recognizing or expressing emotions.
- Trouble coping with stress (may turn to drugs, food, sex).
- Low self-worth/ depression.
- Feeling like damaged goods.
- Troubled relationships and work life.
- Caring "too much" (trying to give the world the love they never had).
- People pleasing and submissive behavior.

- Drugs/alcohol problems.

Research shows that many women who were abused as children tend to be unconsciously drawn to men who are abusive. This research also shows that sexual abusers of children, both male and female, were most likely abused themselves as children.

The cycle can break if a person gets therapeutic help to heal their trauma, understands why they behave as they do, learn new parenting skills, express their feelings, and change their thinking and behavior.

MYTHS about child sexual abuse

Myth: Children will often make up stories about being sexually abused to get attention or to get back at someone.

> Children very rarely make up the abuse. Most children are embarrassed and frightened to talk about the abuse. Younger children may not even understand what the abuse is or what it means, and they do not know what reactions they will get if they tell.

Myth: Children provoke sexual assault by their behavior, because they can be seductive.

> The sole responsibility for any sexual assault rests on the assailants, not the child. Perpetrators often use coercion and force. Children do not ask to be assaulted and abused.

Myth: Children are not able to protect themselves from sexual assaults.

> Children can be taught safety about sexual assault. It is important to teach them what they can do if it happens to them: yell, hit, run, and get help.

Myth: If you talk openly about sexual assault with children it will traumatize them.

> Talking openly with children about sexual assault as a safety issue can help them feel empowered, not traumatized. This way they have the information they need to better protect themselves and get help.

The Healing Process

In their book, *The Courage to Heal*, Ellen Bass and Laura Davis describe the **stages of the healing process**. Although most of these stages are necessary for every survivor, a few of them are not applicable for every person.

Making the Decision to Heal: Once we recognize the effects of sexual abuse in our life, we need to make an active commitment to heal. Deep healing happens only when we choose it and are willing to change ourselves.

The Emergency Stage: Beginning to deal with memories and suppressed feelings can throw our life into utter turmoil. Remember, this is only a stage. It will not last forever.

Remembering: Many survivors suppress all memories of what happened to them as children. Those who do not forget the actual incidents forget how it felt at the time. Remembering is the process of getting back both memory and feeling.

Believing it Happened: Survivors often doubt their own perceptions. Coming to believe that the abuse really happened, and that it really hurt us, is a vital part of the healing process.

Breaking the Silence: Most adult survivors kept the abuse a secret in childhood. Telling another human being about what happened to us is a powerful healing force that can dispel the shame of being a victim.

Understanding that it Wasn't Your Fault: Adult survivors must place the blame where it belongs – directly on the shoulders of the abusers.

Making Contact with the Child Within: Many survivors have lost touch with their own vulnerability. Getting in touch with the child within can help us feel compassion for ourselves, more anger at our abuser, and greater intimacy with others.

Trusting Yourself: The best guide for healing is our own inner voice. Learning to trust our own perceptions, feelings, and intuitions forms a new basis for actions in the world.

Grieving and Mourning: As children being abused, and later as adults, most survivors haven't felt their losses. Grieving is a way to honor our pain, let go, and move into the present.

Anger – the Backbone of Healing: Anger is a powerful and liberating force. Whether we need to get in touch with it or have always had plenty to spare, directing our rage squarely at our abuser, and at those who did not protect us, is pivotal to healing.

Disclosures and Confrontations: Directly confronting our abuser and/or our family is not for every survivor, but it can be a dramatic, cleansing tool.

Forgiveness: Forgiveness of the abuser in not an essential part of the healing process, although it tends to be the most recommended. The only essential forgiveness is for ourselves.

Spirituality: Having a sense of a power greater than ourselves can be a real asset in the healing process. Spirituality is a uniquely personal experience. We might find it through traditional religion, meditation, nature, or our support group.

Resolution and Moving On: As we move through these stages again and again, we will reach a point of integration. Our feelings and perspectives will stabilize. We will come to terms with our abusers and other family members. While we will not erase our history, we will make deep and lasting changes in our life. Having gained awareness, compassion, and power through healing, we will have the opportunity to work toward a better world.

Why Child Abuse?

People that abuse children tend to have low self-worth, poor impulse control, and lack emotional maturity and empathy. Many also abuse drugs and alcohol, and as was mentioned earlier, were abused themselves as children.[5]

The shame for committing child abuse seems to outweigh all other forms of disapproved behaviors – even murder. There are not a lot of straight answers to why child abuse is so prevalent in this culture. Estimates reveal that 1 in 4 girls and 1 out of every 6 boys have been sexually abused as a child. That equates to millions of people. But wouldn't that mean there are also millions who are doing the abusing? What this indicates is that this in not just an individual problem but a social issue as well.

There are certain beliefs we have about children and about sexuality, mostly unconscious, that steer many people to behave abusively towards kids.

> *"The vast majority of people who abuse children were abused themselves as children."*

Our human history is replete with cultures that encouraged sex between children and adults. Some of these cultures still exist today. Could their beliefs still be influencing us to this day? If we were abused as kids, could this be sending the implicit message that this is how children and adults show love, or that sex equals love?

The difference between healthy human touching and sex has been muddled for many, and if you mix that with our culture's unwillingness to teach empathy, emotional intelligence, long-term consequential thinking, and impulse control, you have some of the main ingredients for sexual abuse.

In addition, some of our religious beliefs about sex and anything sexual are replete with shame. Shaming a person for sexual urges and behavior sex just makes them more curious. Shaming anyone for an urge and behavior just makes it more likely to occur. We repress the behavior/urge/quality, pushing it away as fast as possible. But the harder we force it away, the more it resists and pushes back. As these thoughts begin to bubble up in our mind, we get scared and push even harder, using up more and more energy in defense until we become so overwhelmed that it takes us over and we act upon the urge. Then we feel more shame and thus we experience a greater need to deny it or cover it up, and the cycle continues.

The person who feels ashamed of their eating tends to seek consolation in food.
The person who feels shame about their drug habit tends to seek escape in more drugs.
The same seems to be the case for child abuse.

Most perpetrators of abuse have themselves been abused. When the shame of these traumas, in the form of thoughts and feelings, begin to surface, it activates the desperate feelings of *helplessness and powerlessness*, and the person may either re-enact the trauma as a victim or as the perpetrator. Re-enacting as a victim means they will unconsciously get themselves into situations where they will once again be abused. Others will take on the role of the perpetrator as the only way they know how to overcome these agonizing feelings of helplessness and powerlessness. It is about power and control. They are playing out the abuser and victim roles at the same time. And it is the toxic shame of feeling flawed as a person that fuels and perpetuates these actions.

Gershen Kaufman writes in the book, *Shame: The Power of Caring* [28]:

> *"The perpetrator of the assault or violation also is shame based. Such acts are acts of power and revenge, born of impotence and fueled by shame... that scene of forcible violation is a reenactment, a transformation of a scene of equal powerlessness and humiliation experienced by the perpetrator at the hands of a different tormentor... The victim, the target of revenge, is confused with the source of the perpetrator's shame. By defeating and humiliating the victim, the perpetrator is momentarily freed of shame."*

We cannot break the cycle by continuing to shame people, believing they are "bad" or "evil" and "abusers for life." It is the behavior that is shameful not the person's value as a human. And there *is* hope for change.

In no way is it being stated that the person abusing is not responsible for their behavior. There are still <u>consequences</u> to doing harm to children. The *behavior* is wrong, not the person. Change their core beliefs and you change them.

When people are too ashamed to come out and admit to a problem, the issue goes unresolved. When help is not sought, it continues to get passed down. There are a scant amount of agencies and support groups to help people who abuse children.

Healing on a mass scale requires that we let go of shaming people and instead learn and choose to see deeper into others – to see human beings just like us, that have lost their way and need help. This could start a flow for the creation of agencies, research, books, support groups and therapies to help abusers of children release emotions, heal trauma, become aware of their limiting beliefs, develop empathy and impulse control, and make new healthier choices.

Taking the Child Abuse Call:

Example 1: *A child calls asking for help. She has just been abused.*

Secure the child's **safety first**. Get the child away from the attacker and to a safe place. Send medical attention or the police if the child is hurt or is being threatened and wants help.

> *"Are you hurt?"*
> *"Where are you hurt?"*
> *"Do you want me to send help?"*
> *"What is your address?"*
> *"Where is the attacker?"* (a person's name if it is someone she knows)
> *"Is there some place safe you can go?" "A neighbor's house? A room with a door lock?"*
> *"Is there anyone else there with you?"*

Get the child's **name and age.**

We may have to calm the child down in order to find out what is going on.

> *"I can hear that you are really upset. That's okay. I'm here to help you. Can you take a few big, deep breaths with me?"*

If help is on the way, reassure the child that help is coming and **keep them on the line.** Ask Big Picture questions. The more upset the child is, the more the questions should be <u>direct</u> and *less* open-ended to keep the child focused on us. When talking to children do not use the same language and tone as with an adult. The younger the child, the warmer and more caring our voice should sound, but be careful not to talk down to them.

Example 2: *A parent or adult calls after a child has reached out to the crisis line. The parent wants to know who we are and what their child has told us.*

> **Maintain confidentiality**, telling the parent nothing of the conversation. Do not admit to even having spoken to the child. Telling the parent anything could

lead to further damaging repercussions for the child.

> *"I'm sorry but no child has called here this evening."*

Reflect back the parent's feelings.

> *"It sounds like something is really upsetting you. What's going on? Did something happen?"*

There is no guarantee that the parent will calm down or tell you anything, but we can **try to engage the parent in the call** by asking Big Picture questions. Be aware of your judgments though. This is when you will be tested the most. Empathize with the parent's fears and deeper hopes. If we can help the parent, we may be able to prevent future abuse.

Example 3: *Caller reveals abuse from the past.*

For many people a confidential hotline is the first place they will come to disclose they have been abused. The shame may still be too great to talk about face to face, and the feeling of control they have in a telephone conversation is greater than a therapeutic setting. Sometimes a caller will reveal the past abuse, then immediately hang up. Simply telling someone was a big first step.

Our job is to **listen and empathize**. *Validate* and *Normalize* all of their feelings. If they are crying, let them cry. If there is silence, let them have it. Do not push.

> *"It took a lot of courage for you to call tonight."*
> *"It's okay to cry. This must be very difficult for you."*
>
> *"It sounds like you have been holding in a lot of hurt and sadness for a long time."*

If you hear any shame or self-blame:

> **"What happened was not your fault."**
> **"You didn't do anything wrong."**
> **"I know it feels like you did something wrong, but you didn't."**

Get the **Big Picture** with open-ended questions.

> *"How has this been affecting your life?"*
> *"Have you talked to anyone else about this?"*
> *"What made you call* **tonight?"**
> *"When did this occur?"*
> *"How long did it go on for?"*
> *"Does anyone else know?"*

"Are you still in contact with that person (the abuser)?"
"What has been the worst part of this experience for you?"

After you have explored much of the Big Picture, find out about their **history of coping and support.**

"What helps you to feel better?"
"How do you cope with these feelings?"
"Do you have any friends or family you feel comfortable talking to about this?"
"Where else have you sought help?"

Find out if they are ready and willing to start the healing process. Let them know they are not alone and there are many people including ourselves that would like to help. Inform the caller that it takes time, work, and willingness to heal, but it can be done.

After looking at what the caller's **goals** are and how he or she would like to feel, then we can brainstorm ideas. Allow the caller to come up with ideas first, then offer any **suggestions** we may have.

Example 4: *A caller has been abusing his kids.*

Watch for judgments and reach deeper to empathize with the feelings the caller is having. The only way to help the kids is to help the caller in this situation. Shame and judgment do more damage than good. Know that this person is doing the best they can given their level of awareness and life conditions no matter how unhealthy and hurtful their behaviors are. Be curious, seek to understand, and ask Big Picture questions. Ask the names of their kids. This will help them to see the kids more as people rather than objects.

"What are your children's names?"
"What made you call tonight?"
"Are your children hurt right now?"
"How hard do you hit Jimmy and Samantha?"
"When did you first start touching Laura?"
"How do you feel when you touch her?"
"What are you feeling just before touching her?"

Resources and Referrals

- *Therapy/counseling/support groups* are highly recommended.
- *Yesican.org* – Provides information, referrals, and chat rooms for survivors.

- *Child Abuse Hotline.* – Accepts reports of child abuse, offers counseling, referrals and information.
- *The Courage to Heal* – A wonderful book that contains everything you will need to start the healing journey.

Help for Runaways

Runaways are at risk for addiction, AIDS, and prostitution, which may be their only means of survival if they are on the streets for any length of time. Their best hope is to link up as soon as possible with a local organization that can provide temporary shelter and/or counseling to assist them in examining their options.[19]

Empathy and Child Abuse

"Empathy creates an atmosphere of safety, for you know that your concerns will be heard and you will be treated with respect and consideration for your welfare." –Power of Empathy

Journal on any experiences of abuse you had as a child. What were some of your feelings? How has it affected your life? How have you coped thus far? What kind of healing do you feel you still have to do?

Notice any judgments you have toward people who abuse children. Notice judgments you have toward people who are not yet willing to begin the healing process.

Be aware of your urges to fix or rescue the victims or perpetrators of abuse. By accepting them just as they are and also seeing that they have the potential to grow and heal, we create the space for them to release their shame, forgive themselves and others, and make new, healthier choices.

Toward a Deeper Understanding . . .

Forgiveness

"Forgiving releases you from the punishment of a self-made prison where you are both the inmate and the jailer." –Doc Childre and Howard Martin

Forgiveness is the penultimate human ability. And it is the depth of our *empathy* that determines our ability to forgive. Empathy moves us into a deeper and wider understanding of ourselves and others, which opens us into compassion. If we stay in this field of compassion long enough, forgiveness will come forward to release all of our judgments, grievances, and resentments – heal our wounds – dissolve inner and outer boundaries – and allow loving energy to flow through us more fully.

> *"Once there is forgiveness, we are no longer victims of the past.*
> *In knowing who we really are, any memories, no matter how traumatic*
> *they once seemed, are now part of the grace of our lives."* –*Richard Moss*

When we forgive, we do not "forgive and forget." We are still aware of what happened – we learn from it – but we now hold the past within ourselves much differently. No longer are these memories suffused with resentment, anger, hurt, and fear. We may begin to see the past with evolutionary eyes – from the perspective that everything serves the purpose to help us grow and develop.

> *"You will know that forgiveness has begun when you recall those*
> *who hurt you and feel the power to wish them well."* –*Lewis B. Smedes*

We don't let people off the hook; we let *ourselves* off the hook from our judgments. This frees us from the reactive energy and negative emotions, from the inner conflict, from the guilt and shame, and from the past haunting us.

All judgment is ultimately self-judgment. What we judge in others, we first judge in ourselves. What we hate in others, we are currently hating in ourselves. This is why the deepest lasting healing occurs by forgiving ourselves. We forgive ourselves for the judgments we have made against *ourselves.*

> *"Forgiveness is a complex act of consciousness,*
> *one that liberates the psyche and soul from the need for personal*
> *vengeance and the perception of oneself as a victim."* –*Caroline Myss*

Yes, we can ask for God's forgiveness. Yes, we can forgive others who have harmed us. But the most healing forgiveness is that of Self-Forgiveness – for the judgments we have made against ourselves and others.

> *"Forgiveness is the fragrance that the violet sheds on the*
> *heels that has crushed it."* –*Mark Twain*

Forgiveness doesn't mean we now condone certain behaviors. Forgiveness is about holding ourselves, others, and situations in a new way – from a more loving, truthful perspective. We do not need to make amends with people if we don't want to. It doesn't mean we now have to like the people who may have tried to harm us. It doesn't mean we have to trust them either. *We simply release our judgment against them.* We stop harming ourselves and others when we do this and bring love where there was once hate and fear.

Every time we forgive and heal a judgment within us, we are able to be with another with a much greater degree of empathy and compassion. And as crisis workers, this is what we are being called to do.

EMPATHY DEVELOPMENT
Releasing Judgments
Exercise #4

Step 1 is to become aware of what our judgments are.
Step 2 is to become aware of why we judge.
Step 3 is to reinterpret our judgments.
Step 4 is to use relationships as a path to developing empathy.

After the initial honeymoon phase of an intimate relationship, when everything is "lovey dovey," defenses let down, we drop our mask a little, and we begin to find aspects in this other person that trigger us. This is when our judgments start rearing their head. It feels like the other is attacking us by not being the person *we* want them to be. Soon we are caught up in a cycle of resentment and blame as we try to change each other to meet our expectations.

> *"We all attract certain people into our lives who have developed qualities opposite the ones we are most identified with. In other words, they mirror our disowned selves, and we mirror theirs." –Shakti Gawain*

Most of us are not conscious of this process and we end up judging and trying to change our partner in the very ways that we are unconsciously attracted to them. For example, it drives John crazy that Bonnie is so controlling while Bonnie judges John for being too disorganized, flaky, and for doing everything half-assed. This is known as shadow-boxing.

We are attracted to people who express the very qualities we are disowning. Instead of using this as a path to growth and healing, we blame each other, judge each other, and try to change each other. We judge a quality in another because we shame it in ourselves first, and we have been taught that our problems and solutions are outside of us and not within.

> *"Out beyond ideas of wrongdoing and rightdoing, there is a field. I will meet you there." –Rumi*

Part One:

This exercise builds upon the other exercises you have been working on. Pick a **quality** in your partner, close friend, or family member that you feel judgmental about.

Judgment Quality_____

Continue through the judgment exercises that preceded this one until you **reinterpret** the quality you have been cutting off in yourself. This is how you begin to free yourself from reactivity and resentment toward your partner or friend and discover a deeper connection based on empathy.

Reinterpreted Quality_____

If I were to let go of this judgment, I am concerned/afraid that:

_____

_____

If I were to own some of the reinterpreted quality, I am concerned/afraid that:

_____

_____

Part Two:

In his book *On Becoming a Person*, the psychologist Carl Rogers suggests this strategy as a means of testing your listening skills and developing your empathy:

> *"The next time you get into an argument with someone, stop the discussion for a moment and for an experiment, institute this rule. Each person can speak up for himself only after he has **first restated the ideas and feelings of the previous speaker accurately, and to that speaker's satisfaction.** It would be necessary for you to really achieve the other person's frame of reference – **to understand their thoughts and feelings so well that you could summarize them.** Sounds simple, doesn't it? But if you try it you will discover it is one of the most difficult things you have ever tried to do. However, once you have been able to see the other's point of view, your own comments will have to be drastically revised. You will also find the emotion going out of the discussion, the differences being reduced, and those differences which remain being of a rational and understandable sort."*[29]

Talk to your partner or friend or family member. Tell them about the exercise and the possible benefits. Ask them if they would be willing to try this with you. Then, once you find yourself falling into your old pattern of arguing, stop yourself and agree to try this communication exercise.

DOMESTIC VIOLENCE

Statistics

According to the National Coalition Against Domestic Violence (NCADV):[30]

- 1 in 3 women and 1 in 4 men have been victims of some form of physical violence by an intimate partner within their lifetime.
- Approximately 90% of domestic assaults are men against women.
- 1 in 7 women and 1 in 18 men have been stalked by an intimate partner during their lifetime to the point in which they felt very fearful or believed that they or someone close to them would be harmed or killed.
- On a typical day, there are more than 20,000 phone calls placed to domestic violence hotlines nationwide.
- Intimate partner violence accounts for 15% of all violent crime.

Violence occurs in same sex relationships at about the same rate as opposite sex ones.

For ease of communication in this section, the batterer will be referred to as "he" and the victim will be called "she."

What is Abuse?

Abuse can be considered any attempt to control, manipulate, or demean another individual using physical, emotional, or sexual tactics.[31]

Physical Abuse: Any use of size, strength, or presence to hurt or control someone else.

Emotional/Psychological Abuse: Includes insults, threats, coercive tactics, intense jealousy, and criticisms to hurt, terrorize, or control someone. Many battered women describe emotional abuse as equally, if not more, damaging than physical abuse.

Examples of this type of abuse include:
- Humiliating the victim
- Controlling what the victim can or cannot do.
- Withholding information from the victim.
- Isolating the victim from friends and/or family.
- Deliberately doing something to make the victim feel diminished or embarrassed.
- Stalking.
- Demeaning the victim in public or in private.

- Undermining the victim's confidence and/or sense of self-worth.
- Convincing the victim she is crazy.

Sexual Abuse: Forced sex, unwanted touching, withholding sex as punishment, and unfaithfulness are all forms of this type of abuse. It is often used as a means to exert power and to further shame and humiliate someone.

Economic Abuse: Trying to keep someone from getting or keeping a job, making the person ask for money, giving an allowance, or taking money. The batterer will typically handle all finances as a means of control to create further dependence.

The Cycle

According to Lenore Walker, author of *The Battered Woman*, violent relationships are not always violent but, rather, often follow a three-phase cycle.[32]

Phase 1: Tension Building Phase
    Less lethal forms of battering occur during this time. Sensing the tension, the woman will try to placate the abusive partner to prevent the abuse. She will minimize the minor incidents, blame herself for her partner's behavior, and deny that the tension will escalate to more severe battering, even though it may have happened many times before.

Phase 2: The Acute-Battering Phase
    His rage escalates dramatically. Severe injuries occur as a result of the battering and the woman experiences shock and disbelief that the incident has occurred.

Phase 3: The Remorseful Phase
    He expresses contrition over his behavior, offering gifts and promises to change. He begins to elicit feelings of guilt and sympathy from the woman. The woman's desire to believe he will change and his temporarily changed behavior reinforce her desire to stay in the relationship.

This cycle is not a part of all violent relationships. When present, however, the three phases of abuse vary from couple to couple in terms of intensity and length of time. Unless this cycle is broken, the violence will escalate, in both frequency and severity.

Characteristics of One Who Batters

We know that those who perpetrate domestic violence come in all shapes and sizes, professions, educational backgrounds, religious affiliations, and ethnic backgrounds. However, they do have some characteristics in common: [31]

Low Self-Worth Feelings of shame and inferiority are overcompensated for by attempting to dominate the woman. These feelings are usually masked behind a cool guy, tough guy, or gentleman persona.

Dual Personality Typically described as a Jekyll and Hyde personality, he can be charming and loving as well as hostile and violent. He idealizes as well as devalues his partner. The woman spends much of her time trying to be the perfect wife so he will maintain his loving side.

Jealousy Monitoring, constantly checking up on, controlling and manipulating the woman's behavior all result from his lack of trust and fear of abandonment. He believes if he can completely control her, she will not leave him.

Feelings of Anxiety and Depression These feelings manifest from an intense fear of abandonment, guilt, and shame.

Selfish/Needy He wants everything his way. Only *his* feelings are important. He expects her to take care of his every need.

Defensive/Blaming Typically he will not accept responsibility for his actions and instead resorts to rationalizing, denial, and blame. He is usually hypersensitive to the slightest criticism so his defenses are always up. He blames everyone else for all his problems especially his partner, who he will blame as the cause of the abuse. He may even deny the abuse ever took place, cueing the woman to question her own judgments and realities.

Belief in the Use of Violence He commonly believes that women are inferior and should be subservient to men. He also believes that marriage gives him unrestricted control of his wife and that violence is an acceptable form of conflict resolution. These are learned in his home as a child and supported in large part by our society.

Some people erroneously believe that the man who batters is out of control. Typically when the police arrive on the scene, he is extremely calm. He will only smash *her* things, and he almost always waits until he is home to explode on her. However, some abusers do have what are called '**redouts**' where they do not remember any part of the explosion.

Other signs of a battering personality:

- Quick involvement. They come on strong, needing someone desperately.
- Verbal abuse which depersonalizes the victim as a way to rationalize assaults. Erodes her self-esteem as a means of keeping her dependent.
- Past battering.
- Breaking or striking objects.
- Low impulse control.
- Low frustration tolerance.

- Treats partner like a possession.
- Drinks or uses drugs excessively.
- Was abused as a child or saw his father abuse his mother.

Characteristics of the Battered Woman

Domestic violence crosses all socioeconomic, ethnic, racial, educational, age, and religious lines for the abused. Some of the common characteristics of the battered woman include:

Low Self-Worth and Self-Esteem   Part of the problem lies in that she has internalized many of the gender stereotype beliefs in our society, which say that women are inferior. Living with ongoing devaluation from her partner begins to take its toll, eroding her self-worth even more.

Guilt   The batterer works hard to convince the woman that the abuse is her fault, and she increasingly accepts responsibility for his abusive actions. She thinks, if only she can be a better wife, mother, lover, etc. This gives her a sense of control, but in reality she has no control over his behavior, and eventually failure after failure contributes to her lowered sense of self. She is not allowed to express her feelings, and so they get turned inward and are manifested as guilt and shame. Religious beliefs may also play a role in feelings of guilt.

Helplessness   Women who are beaten down time after time begin to feel like there is no way out and no hope of ever getting out. They adopt the survival strategies of passivity, submissiveness, dependency and an inability to act or even think. Sometimes the only sense of control in an impending abuse situation is to push his buttons and get the abuse over with.

Denial   Often the terror and anger can be too much, so denial becomes the coping mechanism. She denies that the abuse ever occurred, denies that he is responsible, and that she would be able to survive without him. She believes that she is the instigator of the abuse, that he is a good man, and that she deserves the punishment.

Feelings of fear   The abused woman is in a constant state of terror. She fears being hit, yelled at, of him hurting others, of abandonment, and of criticism from others if she leaves. She is confused and constantly hyper-vigilant as to who he is today and when the next explosion will occur.

Why do they batter?

"Violence increases the man's feelings of insecurity since it also increases the risk that his partner will leave or grow distant from him. He typically reacts to these possibilities with more violence. His violence is self-perpetuating unless it is directly confronted." –K.J.Wilson

We have already discussed that his behaviors stem from a desire to control and manipulate his partner based on a deep fear of abandonment. He holds an enormous amount of shame inside and believes in traditional sex role stereotypes, such as men are superior to women and that violence is an acceptable means of resolving conflicts. He is able to silence an argument or control a situation seemingly without any consequences.[5]

These factors play a huge role in the pervasiveness and perpetuation of domestic violence. But what about childhood? Is there something that occurs in the man's upbringing that has an effect on his later abuse behaviors?

The Man Who Batters and his Father

Typically, the father is also a violent man who relied on hitting as a way to resolve conflicts in their family. He is often cold as well as verbally and physically abusive to the boy for not living up to expectations: *"You'll never amount to anything. You're no good."* Shame and low self-worth is the result for the son.

The boy feels *powerless* and *terrified* in the face of his father, and at the same time *angry* and *rageful*. His model for behavior and dealing with his feelings came from this man. His greatest fear is of being rejected and abandoned. He constantly fears attack and attempts to cope by being defensive or by blaming and criticizing others to take the light off of himself.

The Man Who Batters and his Mother

Early in development the child begins to separate from the mother, who has to be able balance the closeness and separateness that the child needs. But if mom has trouble with this early phase, and she is cold or rejecting in any way, the child will feel shame, which may become ingrained deeply into the conditioned mind. He may become *anxious about being rejected again and angry that she has power over him*. He later generalizes these feelings into his relationships and unconsciously looks to work things out and make it right.

It becomes a big push/pull. He wants love so much – the unconditional love he never got – and this makes him scared to be too distant. But he is also afraid to get too close, fearing another rejection, so he feels it necessary to control the emotional distance of the relationship. He seeks out a woman to dominate and manipulate to suit these needs.

134

He could not trust mom, so he now lacks trust in all women. This leads to the jealousy, accusations, and monitoring that play such a big part of abusive relationships. He attempts to make her dependent upon him to regain a sense of power and make sure she does not abandon him.

When he begins to feel intimate and vulnerable with her, it builds a tension of impending doom. He believes that she is making him feel this way. Everything is blown out of proportion as a rejection. Tension builds more and more until finally he explodes, and just like his father, he uses physical force to gain his power back and quell the problem.

He has never grown up emotionally. The loud shouting is really just the crying and wailing of a young child, smashing objects is shaking the crib, and punching is the child thrashing about. His emotional instability and actions are strikingly similar to that of a Borderline Personality Type.

> *"Deep down even the most hardened criminal is starving for the*
> *same thing that motivates the innocent baby:*
> *Love and acceptance" –Lily Fairchilde*

Why does she stay?

Battered women have so often been blamed for their abusive situations, citing reasons such as: she unconsciously enjoys the abuse, she is emotionally and mentally unstable, she does things to cause the battering, and it is because she grew up in an abusive family. *These are all myths.* **The victims are not to blame**. They do not enjoy the abuse, they typically are not mentally and emotionally unstable, they do not "cause" the abuse, and many did not grow up in abusive households.

As with battering behavior, there are many factors that come together to keep a woman feeling stuck in a cycle of abuse.

> **Learned Helplessness**: He has manipulated and eroded her self-worth and self-esteem to practically nothing. She believes she is too stupid or incompetent to be able to change things or leave. She feels *powerless, helpless, hopeless, depressed and feels that no one can help her*. She often becomes numb to the physical punishment.
>
> **Beliefs in Gender Role Stereotypes**: She believes that men are superior and that her role is to obey them. His possessiveness is seen as proof of his love. She may also think that marriage gives him the right to use force and that violence is an acceptable means of resolving problems. Other beliefs include the duty to keep the family together and that the health of the relationship is a direct reflection on her.

Dependence: He manipulates her life so that she becomes dependent upon him, financially, emotionally, psychologically, physically. He beats her down and may make threats about others close to her if she leaves. He is seen as omnipotent.

Kids: If there are kids involved, she may fear losing the kids in a court battle. She may also believe that she has to keep the family together for the sake of the children, even though this violence proves to be more harmful for them.

Contrition: The contrition phase can be extremely powerful. He will buy her flowers and gifts, make her promises. He will portray himself as wounded and lost, hungering for love, needing someone to take care of him. It brings out the rescuer in her, thinking she can save him. He will often say things such as, *"You and me against the world"* and *"We can beat this together." "I promise I'll change." "It's because I love you." "It's only to save you from yourself".* She thinks, *"Maybe this time he means it."*

Media: This culture often sends out messages telling women that they need a man to be happy or even to survive. This is one of the central messages in the Cinderella story and its many offshoots.

Family: If violence was modeled in her family, she may believe it is normal. Also, if her father treated her like a fragile doll, she may believe she is incapable of taking care of herself.

> *"If you receive disrespect, look to yourself and ask that*
> *most important question, 'Why have I allowed myself*
> *to be treated this way?' instead of, 'Why are they*
> *doing this to me again?'"* –Wayne Dyer

What it boils down to is a myriad of factors that contribute to her belief that either she will not be able to survive without him, or he will not let her survive without him. She fears that no one will believe her. Sometimes she does not even know if she believes herself.

Taking the domestic violence call

> *"Helping a battered woman is a process that may*
> *take a long time. We have to realize that she needs*
> *to move according to her own timetable and not*
> *ours."* –Erin Clarke, Austin Center for Battered Women

Safety is our number one concern!

If we receive any direct or indirect hint that someone might be in danger, do not hesitate to ask about their <u>safety</u>.

> *"Are you okay?"*
> *"Are you hurt?"*
> *"Do you want me to send some help?"*
> *"Where are you?"*
> *"Is there anyone else there?"*

If they want the police or medical attention to be sent, get their **information.**

> *"What is your address?"*
> *"What is your name?"*
> *"What is your phone number?"*

Let them know help is on the way and **keep them on the phone until help arrives.** If they are in immediate danger, it may be best to <u>**get them to a safe place**</u>.

> *"Are you safe right now?"*
> *"Where is he right now?"*
> *"When is he coming back?"*
> *"Is there anyone else there with you?"*
> *"Is there a room you can go to where you can lock the door and be safe until help arrives?"*
> *"Is there a friend or neighbor's house you can go to right now?"*
> *"Do you want to go to a shelter?"*

Come up with a **trigger word** with her to let you know when he comes home. This is so he does not suspect she is on the phone calling for help.

Ask if she has **any children**. Find out their ages and genders. Some shelters will not allow boys older than a certain age.

> *"Do you have any children?"*
> *"Are the kids with him?"*
> *"Are the kids safe right now?"*
> *"Has he ever hit the children?"*

If there are no immediate safety concerns, <u>it is time to listen</u>. Let her tell her story while <u>Perception Checking</u>.

> *"So what I hear you saying is that your husband is not letting you go out with your friend this weekend and this seems to be a pattern of his. You feel upset about this, lonely, and afraid to speak up about this issue. Is this accurate?"*

Gather the **Big Picture**.

> *"Does your partner threaten or criticize you?"*
> *"What kinds of things does he say?"*
> *"How do you feel about that?"*
> *"Does your partner try to control your behavior by telling you where you can go or who you can associate with?" "How so?"*
> *"Is your partner extremely possessive or jealous?"*
> *"How do you feel about that?"*
> *"What happens when you and your partner fight or disagree?"*
> *"Has your partner ever physically hurt or threatened you?"*
> *"Your kids?"*
> *"How do you feel about that?"*
> *"How long has this been going on for?"*
> *"How often does he hit you?"*
> *"What made you call tonight?"*

Explore her feelings empathically with <u>validation and normalization</u>. **Reflect** how she is coming across to you in order to help her identify her feelings.

> *"This must be really hard for you."*
> *"It sounds like you are really angry at him for hitting you."*
> *"I know you are scared right now. That's okay. I'm here to help you."*
> *"You sound really angry and hurt right now. I know I would feel that way if my partner threatened me."*

This is an easy situation to get caught up in your own personal reactions. Blaming, judging, and condemning the perpetrator for his actions and/or the victim for not leaving or for protecting him are not going to be helpful. We will quickly lose rapport and the chance to really help. Saying things like, *"Why don't you just leave?"* or *"Why do you put up with it?"* or even *"Why do you let him do that to you?"* come across as belittling with the undertone that this is her fault. Notice your reactions, and then choose instead to listen empathically and with curiosity. **Let her know that it is *not* her fault.**

> *"You don't deserve to be treated that way."*
> *"No one, not even your husband, has the right to do that to you."*
> *"It's not your fault."*

Focus on the man's *behavior* and not him. If we focus on him, the woman may become defensive and try to make excuses for him. Battered women often express love for their abusive partners. They may hate his abusive behaviors and know he can be dangerous, yet still have feelings for him.

> *"I'm really concerned about the way John treats you sometimes."*
>
> *"It sounds like you are angry with the way he treats you sometimes,*

but you still have strong feelings for him. It's okay to feel conflicted about this."

"It sounds like a part of you wants to leave, a part of you is scared to leave, and another part still loves him. Is this accurate?"

Don't give advice. Let her tell us what she needs rather than assuming we know what is best for her. If we try to rescue her by giving her advice, we are actually setting her up to feel like she has disappointed us if she does not do what we have told her. These feelings may prevent her from reaching out to us again in the future. Rescuing her also just reinforces her helplessness. Support her in making her own decisions.

Allow her to tell her story. **Just be there for her with support.** Let her know you believe her and want to hear about her experiences. Convey to her that you care and that you are concerned about her safety.

"I'm really concerned about your safety and wonder what's going to happen to you if this hitting doesn't stop."

Be aware of any frustration or anger you feel toward her if she does not want to leave. She may fear retaliation. The highest risk or injury is right after she leaves or threatens to leave. Remember, there is a lot that goes into leaving. She may be leaving the home with almost nothing but the clothes on her back, the kids will be confused, they may have to change schools, and she may have to quit her job.

"We are here for you when you are ready to leave."

Ask her if she is interested in a safety plan to help protect her and her kids from future violence.

"Is there anywhere you can go where you will be safe?"
"Friends?" "Family?"

- She can ask the neighbors to call the police if they hear any violence.
- Teach the kids to dial 911.
- Come up with a code word for the family to know it's time to go to a safe place and possibly call 911.
- Have a room for her to get away. Stay away from rooms with weapons.
- Identify in advance any doors, windows, or stairways that would allow her to get out of the house quickly and safely.

If she is open to the idea of eventually leaving for good, **explore a safe plan with her.**

"Have you ever threatened to leave?"
"How did he react?"

Leaving the abusive partner requires an incredible amount of planning and secrecy and can be very dangerous. There must be a commitment not only to ending the abusive relationship, but to severing ties with almost everything and everyone familiar.

Part of the plan will involve **securing necessities** to take with her as well as **mobilizing some support** when she needs it. She will need to:

- Memorize important phone numbers.
- Keep change for the phone or a pre-paid phone card. (He may not let her have a cell phone.)
- Save money. The more the better. Cash is best.
- Open her own bank account that he doesn't know about. Do not use old checks, ATM, or credit cards. They can be traced.
- Get to know neighbors and keep friends in touch. Have one trusted contact person.
- Keep keys and changes of clothes at a friend or relative's place.
- Gather all important documents in one easy to get to place:
    - ✓ Birth certificates.
    - ✓ School and medical records.
    - ✓ Bank records, lease/mortgage papers.
    - ✓ Passports, green cards, social security cards.
    - ✓ Insurance papers.
    - ✓ Address and phone number books.
    - ✓ Welfare I.D. number.
    - ✓ Any restraining orders, marriage papers.
- Go about life as usual so he does not suspect anything.
- A toy or two for the kids.

Rehearse this escape plan with her when one is established.

Encourage her to **talk to a lawyer.** There are many ways someone can track you down. A lawyer or legal advocate can help with the process.

Discuss domestic violence and the common abusive behaviors associated with it. Inform her that this is about power and control and that it is not going to stop. It will only get worse and could lead to her being killed. His promises of change are just more manipulation. Discuss what *healthy* relationships are like.

Explore the **consequences of staying or leaving**, including that kids are more negatively affected by violence in the home than by being without a father.

Explore all the reasons she stays and the beliefs behind these reasons. Respect all of her values and customs. Often these situations pose huge spiritual/religious dilemmas for abused women. Divorce may not be permitted in their religion, or they are taught to be submissive and devoted to the husband no matter what. She may also believe if she were to obey him, there would not be a need for violence. At a much deeper level, she may believe that somehow she deserves to be abused.

Ask about her **support system**. Encourage her to turn to other people she can trust.

"Who else can you talk to about this?"

If she is only hinting at wanting out but is currently too scared (from threats or dependency), do not press her. Let her know we are available if she would like to talk.

Summary of what to do:
- If she is in immediate danger, get her someplace safe (shelter, relative, friend/neighbor, police station).
- If she wants to leave but is not in immediate danger, work on the plan and mobilizing her support systems.
- Provide information to her about domestic violence, empower her to see that she can do it, and tell her there are people including us that are here to help. Give her all the resources and options available to her, including her right to legal interaction.
- Keep emphasizing that it is not her fault.
- Decrease her feelings of helplessness and dependency.

If a man who batters reaches out to the crisis line . . .

Listen and empathize with his underlying pain. His fears of abandonment, the shame and anger toward himself. Find out what his deepest hope is. Help him to take responsibility for his actions and to realize that it is up to him to change. He can make small steps to learn how to control his anger better and resolve conflicts and painful feelings in a manner more conducive to what he is hoping for.

Do not judge him. This only incurs more shame, which leads to more anger that is going to be turned outward onto the wife. *Help him to see choices and consequences, other ways to get what he really wants. Let him know that there is help. Empower him the best that you can.* The best way to help the endless victims of abuse is to prevent it from happening in the first place. Punishment with jail time or through judgment has not been an effective deterrent to the enormous problem of violence in this country.

If he wants help managing aggressive impulses, **provide him with information, resources, referrals, and other options.**

Acknowledge his courage and willingness to reach out and seek help.

"If we could read the secret history of our enemies,
we would find in each person's life sorrow and suffering
enough to disarm all hostility." –Henry Wadsworth Longfellow

__Elder Abuse__

Caring for elderly people who are mentally impaired can be frustrating, especially for caregivers without proper equipment or skills. One out of every twenty older Americans may be victims of abuse each year. Reporting the abuse of elderly people follows the same basic guidelines for reporting child abuse. Our job is not only to help the elderly victims of the abuse, but to help the caretakers who are often doing the abusing.

Offer the caregivers information and referrals for support groups, education on mental impairments, and getting a rest or respite care.

Assist them in working through feelings of *guilt and resentment*. Also help them deal with any other life stressors. Sometimes the caregiver is a family member who was abused as a child, and this is the only way they know how to deal with frustration. The dependency of an elder may exacerbate any other difficulties people are having in their lives. Many states provide training and support groups for caregivers.

Public guardianship programs, financial planning, and transportation are just a few services available to help the elderly become more autonomous and to be taken care of by people who are closely monitored.[20]

Resources and Referrals

Shelters. Emergency and transitional shelters provide a safe haven, confidential refuge, food, individual and group counseling, parenting skills, job skills training, legal assistance, and help moving toward independent housing. Check to see if the shelter takes children and boys over a certain age.

Support Groups. It can be very healing to gather and share similar experiences, to realize we are not alone, and that our problems are not individual but also social, political and cultural.

Counseling. Counseling is *only* recommended on an *individual* basis. Women who have been battered will justifiably fear retribution by the man who battered her if she talks freely about relationship issues in a couples counseling session.[5]

Couples counseling is only suggested *after* the violence has ceased, the perpetrator completes a domestic violence program, and the counselor has discussed safety issues with the woman.

Hotlines. There are a growing number of hotlines like the National Domestic Violence Hotline that provide information, referrals, crisis intervention, and resource materials to victims of abuse.

Anger management courses. Look on the internet for current class availability on-line or in the caller's area of residence.

Toward a Deeper Understanding . . .

Gender Roles

For thousands of years men and women have been acting out traditional gender roles. Men are the active, protectors and providers of society. They are the warriors and are expected to show no weakness. Women are the passive receivers, the nurturers and caretakers of society. Men are considered dominant and superior, making all the important decisions. Their women are expected to obey.

However, in the last 50 or so years and with the advent of the Industrial Revolution and the Age of Information, the roles have started to become a bit hazier. Women are seeking to assert themselves in all areas of life – the workplace, sports, raising children on their own – and some men are beginning to embrace their more feminine qualities of compassion, empathy, and nurturance. Women seem to be open to these changes much more than men are right now, and this is causing some resistance and conflict.

In truth we all have the capacity for both energies, the yin and the yang, the masculine and the feminine. In childhood however, we are told that only certain qualities are acceptable for our particular gender. So we cut off the other half of us and spend the rest of our lives unconsciously seeking to reconnect with that lost energy through relationships. We are attracted to people who mirror these disowned parts of ourselves. It feels whole to be with that person, and it feels like we have lost a part of ourselves when we part with them.

The problems start because the very qualities we are attracted to, unconsciously, we are also critical of. We have denied those parts of ourselves because we are afraid and ashamed of them and eventually we try to change the other person we are in relationship with. The more extreme the imbalance (hyper-masculine or hyper-feminine), the more we will be attracted to the opposite extreme, thus the more energy we are in conflict with. Each person is trying to change the other, yet scared to leave at the same time. What we do not accept in another, is what we really do not accept in ourselves.

> *"The world is our mirror and will tell us exactly what we are
> cutting off in ourselves through our judgments."*

When we feel cut off, we experience a lack, then we feel the need to fill that lack, and we will strive to fill those needs by trying to control and manipulate our partner and the world. This takes up a lot of energy. We also live with the constant fear of not being enough.

The key is to integrate these energies, both masculine and feminine. Use your judgments and projections, especially in relationships, to become aware of what you are cutting off in yourself. Reinterpret these qualities and integrate them by practicing them in your life and making new choices. Do it slowly, but be persistent and patient. It takes time and work to change old patterns, but it's worth it. Your relationships will improve and so will your health, vitality, and happiness. Do not take our word for it. Try it for yourself.

Empathy and Domestic Violence

"Often what we think is best for others is distorted by our
attachment to our opinions. We want others to be happy
in the way we think they should be happy. It is only
when we want nothing for ourselves that we are
able to see clearly into other's needs and understand how
to serve them. –Gandhi

Journal about any experiences you have had with abuse. How did you feel? How did you react? How does it still affect you today? What would you have wanted from people in those situations in order to help you best cope?

Notice any feelings of judgment that arise within you toward a person who abuses another. Relate to the pain they are in – the hurt, the fear (of abandonment). Know that all of us have had feelings of anger and rage, and even thoughts of violence. Many of us have even acted out violent behaviors. Remember, empathizing with a person doesn't mean we condone their behaviors.

Empathize with the woman's fear of leaving. Know that you too have feared leaving situations that you did not really want to be in anymore. Empathize with how difficult it is to leave a relationship.

Journal on some of your beliefs about men and women's roles. How do some of the underlying beliefs currently influence your personality and behavior.

Be aware that our parents are also doing they best they can. Blaming them for our misery and current life situation is not taking responsibility. Our parents may have had a huge effect on our lives, but ultimately it is up to us to make changes. Blaming and playing the victim does absolutely nothing. Accepting what they did and how they raised us does not mean we have to like what was done. We may have been victimized but we are not victims.

RAPE and SEXUAL ASSAULT

Statistics

- 1 in 5 women and 1 in 71 men have been raped in their lifetime.[33]
- Only 36% of those raped, will report it.[33]
- 80% of rapes are by someone the survivor knows.[33]

What is Rape?

Rape is any type of forced sexual contact without consent between two or more people, regardless of sexual or marital status. The sexual contact may involve the sex organs of one or both, including penetration, however slight, of the vagina or anus or mouth by a penis, hand, or other object.[5]

Rape is a crime of violence. It is not an act of sexual gratification, but an angry and violent expression of a desire to dominate, control, and hurt someone else using sex as a weapon. Most rapes involve a female victim. Men are raped too, although they rarely report it for fear of having their masculinity and sexuality questioned.[5]

An assault can completely upend a person's beliefs that the world is a safe place, that they are in control of their sexuality and their body, and that they know who to trust. Rape is not sex; it is a life-threatening act. Incest is not sex; it is betrayal.

The Truth about Rape

- Rape can be committed by anyone – a stranger, family member, acquaintance, a date, a marital partner.
- 82% of rapes are premeditated and 70% are preceded by some conversation.
- Regardless of marital or social relationship, if a person does not consent to having sex, they are being sexually assaulted.

No one asks to be raped or sexually assaulted. If she wore something low-cut or tight, was acting sexy, went out alone, stayed out late, was drunk, was using drugs, or was kissing her attacker, that does not mean she asked for it. People have a right to be safe from a sexual attack at any time, any place, and under any circumstance. Offenders, not survivors, must be held responsible.[34]

Responses of a Rape Survivor

Everyone's response to a sexual assault is unique. One of the more common responses is **shock.** The survivor may *disbelieve or deny* that the rape ever occurred. This reaction provides an emotional time-out in order to process the experience. This is normal, but if it lasts for more than a few days, it may become detrimental to the healing.

Other common responses include *mood swings, anger, fear and jumpiness, humiliation, feeling dirty and degraded, disrupted eating and sleeping patterns, nightmares, and feeling lucky to be alive.* She may talk a lot and express a myriad of feelings or she may try to maintain control and composure, downplaying her fear, sadness, anxiety, and anger. She may also feel that she was somehow responsible for the rape.

<u>Social consequences</u> include:
- Increased distrust toward others, especially men.
- Short temper, anger, and hostility.
- Breaks into tears easily.
- Wants to be with others constantly.
- Feels the need to get away.

<u>Psychological Consequences</u> include:
- Depression.
- Guilt & Shame.
- Loss of Self-Worth.
- Panic attacks.
- General paranoia.
- Fear of safety and loss of control.

Rape survivors are nine times more likely to attempt suicide than the general population.

<u>Sexual Consequences</u> include:
- Physical pain during sex.
- Difficulty relaxing or feeling indifferent to sex.
- Desiring sex all the time.

The survivor may be concerned about her partner's reaction to her. Current statistics indicate that about half of all survivors lose their love relationships within a year of sexual assault. Survivors may feel the need to exert more control in a relationship than they did prior to the assault. Never push her into having sex before she feels ready.

<u>Physical Consequences</u> include:
- Gynecological/ Genital problems.
- Pain/Wounds from the beating.
- Sexually transmitted diseases.
- Pregnancy.

Taking the Rape call:

Safety is our first concern with any sexual assault call.
- Find out if someone is hurt or is in danger.
- Make sure to **help her get to a safe place** – away from the attacker.

> *"Are you hurt?"*
> *"Are you safe now?"*
> *"Is he coming back?"*
> *"Where is the attacker?"*
> *"Where are you?"*
> *"Is there somewhere you can go . . . away from the attacker?"*
> *"Can you go to room with a door lock or a window?"*
> *"Do you want me to send some help?"*

If they want us to send the police or medical attention, get their **information.**

> *"Where are you?"*
> *"What is the address?"*
> *"What is the phone number you are calling from?"*
> *"What is your name?"*

Once help is on the way, keep her on the phone until they arrive.

If she is crying or in a state of panic, we can help to calm her with some deep breathing or one of the other strategies in the anxiety regulation section of the manual. <u>**Never say "calm down" or "relax."**</u> Those are the words the perpetrator probably said as he tried to rape her. Learn different ways to help people calm down without saying calm down or relax. **Reflect** back her feelings to help her dissolve the intensity of her feelings and let her know we are here to help.

> *"I can hear that you are very upset right now, that's okay. I'm here to help you. Take a few deep breaths with me right now so I can better understand what is going on."*

This can be a very emotional call and it is our job to let the caller express all of her feelings.

Notice your judgments. These calls can engender strong feelings within us and can lead us to making snap judgments like, *"You didn't lock your door?" "What were you thinking walking alone there at night?"* Many men will jump to outrage and get protective: *"I'll kill him."* Sometimes this anger is too much for the survivor, who just dealt with another angry man.

Validate and normalize her feelings. Let her know that all of her reactions and feelings are normal and okay, including her anger. Remember to let her know that <u>it was not her fault</u>. Help her to redirect any anger she has – toward the rapist, not herself.

> *"That must have been terrifying for you. I can see how you would feel too scared to leave the house right now."*

> *"I know I would be angry if someone I trusted did that to me."*

Preserving Evidence

If the victim has just been raped, and she wants to press charges, an examination and evidence collection is essential.

> **Suggest to her not to bathe, brush her teeth, or change clothing.** Semen or anything else from the perpetrator may still be on her and could be used as evidence. She may feel dirty and want to wash it all off. She may also just want all of this to go away. Try to get her to see that this is a normal reaction, but that very often people change their minds later about reporting and then have no evidence to do so. This gives her the option. This could also prevent him from ever doing it again to her or someone else. Stains on clothing, under fingernails, hairs, etc. can also be used as evidence.

> **Urge her to have a medical exam done**. Ask the hospital or rape crisis center to perform a <u>rape kit exam</u>. If she thinks she was drugged, ask to have a urine test as well. The test will gather evidence and test for any wounds, STDs, and pregnancy.

> **Encourage her to report it to a rape crisis center or a police station.**
> Some studies have shown that reporting to police and testifying, though painful, actually help women recover. It also raises the chances of preventing the perpetrator from doing it again.

Have her tell you as much **detail about the incident** as she can, and **have her write it down.** If she waits too long, she may not remember as clearly. It will also work in favor of evidence. Do not force her to talk about it. It is her choice. All you can do is listen, believe her, provide her with information and possible consequences, and encourage her to take positive action to ensure her safety.

Even if the rape or assault occurred a long time ago, it is never too late to get help. Some people erroneously believe that trying to forget about it by keeping busy or suppressing the emotions will make it go away in time. True, it does take time to heal, but the emotional wounds do not heal by themselves. Some inner work must be done. Inner work can involve talking to trusted others, support groups, a therapist, journaling, and reading about how others have dealt with this.

Get the Big Picture by finding out more about her life and her resources.

"Have you talked to anyone else about this?"
"Who would you feel comfortable talking to about this?"
"How have you been coping thus far?"
"How do you usually handle stress or trauma?"
"Is this the first time you have been assaulted?"
"What else is going on in your life right now? Any other problems?"
"What part of the incident had the biggest impact for you?"
"How has this been affecting your life? Your relationships?"

Other ways to help:

- Educate her as to normal reactions of a sexual assault.
- Keep reminding her it is not her fault. No matter what, the offender is always to blame.
- Identify some of her strengths. How does she view her own ability to cope?
- Help her to understand that she is the same person she was before the rape. Let her know that she is still lovable and that she is not damaged.
- It is normal to want to rescue the rape survivor, but it is not helpful to become over-protective of her. Instead, help her rebuild her own internal sense of security by expressing confidence in her coping skills. It is crucial that she learn to be independent again. It just takes time and work. Let her know *she has control now* in her choices of what to do.
- **Offer referrals**, especially to a sexual assault center. They will provide hospital accompaniment, advocacy with police and/or medical personnel, and referrals to other community services as needed. These are free services and some even provide some free counseling and support groups for survivors and their families.

With time and work, healing a sexual assault trauma can help a person grow to be stronger, more compassionate of others, and more loving toward oneself.

Don't Become a Victim

- Do not accept beverages, including non-alcoholic ones, from someone you do not know or trust.
- Always watch your drink at bars and parties. Never leave it unattended.
- Go with other people to parties and leave together.
- Do not allow yourself to be isolated with someone you do not know or trust.
- Clearly state your limits.
- Trust your feelings about a person (gut, intuition).
- Do not walk alone at night, in alleys, etc.
- Learn self-defense.
- Carry protection: mace, pepper spray, etc.
- Project an aura of confidence and strength.

EMPATHY DEVELOPMENT

Awareness #5

Nothing Lasts.

As obvious as this truth seems, most of us don't live it. We humans clutch and grab and attach ourselves to just about anything that brings us a little temporary comfort and security. This may be the most human thing we do. Yet it creates so much suffering.

We hold onto relationships that are no longer healthy, jobs we don't like, and behaviors that no longer serve us. We become so afraid that without our money and possessions, status, beliefs, and self-image, we will not be okay. So we hold on for dear life.

> *"The outer form is a temporary reflection of what you are within, in your essence. That is why love and beauty can never leave you, although all outer forms will." –Eckhart Tolle*

It is our self-judgments and the shame they create that cause us to feeling lacking, unlovable, bad, and unworthy. We then search outside of ourselves for things and people to make us feel happier, safer, whole, and free of these feelings. But these things will never fill us up or remove these feelings. They are things, and they don't last.

Can you feel this need in yourself? The desire to hold on? The desire to get something, believing it will bring you lasting peace, happiness, safety, and freedom? Can you feel the suffering this causes? Can you just be with these feelings? The yearning? The need to control? The fear of loss? The powerlessness of needing something in order to feel better? Can you allow these feelings into your heart?

> *"It is said an Eastern monarch once charged his wise men to invent him a sentence to be ever in view, and which should be true and appropriate in all times and situations. They presented him the words: And this, too, shall pass away." – Abraham Lincoln*

Even we won't last. One day our body will stop working, our mind will shut down, and we will die. If we believe we are only our bodyminds – our mind, body, and personality, then we will spend our entire lives terrified of dying, looking for anything to assuage this despair and terror. This fear is buried so deep that most of us are not aware of it, but it is a huge guiding force in our lives.

A deepened empathy can attune to this holding on, these attachments, the fear, despair, anger, yearning, resentment, and the suffering that is created from the belief that permanent acceptance, safety, and comfort can be found in the external world.

Welcome these feelings, validate and normalize them, sit with them for a while, feel into what it is like to be human, feel into what it is like to be with another human, suffering just like you. Discover the wisdom that naturally arises within this empathic space.

SUICIDE

*"Suicide is a permanent solution to a
temporary problem." –Phil Donahue*

Overwhelming, unmanageable, and interminable SUFFERING. This is what a person who contemplates, attempts, or commits suicide is feeling. They believe that:

- They have tried every possible way to find relief and have failed miserably.
- No one can help them.
- Suicide is the only possible solution.

They want to be **released** from the enormous pressures, burdens, disappointments and hurt they carry around, from the unbearable flow of consciousness the critical, judging mind creates, and from the utter despair of existence. They want relief.

*"For what is suicide but an action to put an end
to intolerable emotions" –Henry A. Murray*

Just having a solution, finally, releases the pressures for many, engendering feelings of happiness. For others, it is a last desperate plea to have acknowledged the incredible pain they are in. And in some cases it is an angry assault on those people who will be left behind to deal with the emotional aftermath.

Leading up to suicide, a person will almost always be severely depressed, experiencing feelings of sadness, anger, and anxiety. Over time many lose interest in their normal activities and some will withdraw from the world altogether, dreading life, carrying huge amounts of *shame and hurt*, which can turn into a feeling of being dead inside.

Making wills, giving stuff away, talking about death a lot, and buying a weapon are overt signs that a person is thinking about suicide. Risk taking or rowdy behavior such as unprotected sex, crime, drugs, alcohol, etc. is common when a person does not care about the consequences of their life anymore.

The suicidal mind is negative and pessimistic to the point of utter *hopelessness*. The constriction and rigidity of their perception often narrows dangerously down to a belief in having only one option left (or in the case of calling the crisis line – two). Recalling and seeing negative experiences seems to be all they are capable of, while coming up with any future plans feels like a wasted effort.

A person who is suicidal has two voices in their head. One that wants to die and to be released from their suffering, and one that desperately wants to live, love, care, and be happy. Although the first voice is much louder and becomes dominant, the latter voice will undoubtedly cry out, leaving little hints and clues for people to pick up on.

The predominant feelings, thoughts, and beliefs are:

Helplessness: Feeling alone and afraid, beaten down, and *powerless* to the forces of society. They do not know what else to do.
Hopelessness: They feel they have tried everything. Nothing new will work, and no one can help them.
Worthlessness: Filled with shame, they feel like a failure who is unworthy of love, life, and even help.

> ***"Darkness, however terrible, never fully***
> ***extinguishes the spark of light."*** *–Deepak Chopra.*

STATISTICS:

Suicide is a lonely act – a desperate and almost always unnecessary one. Most of us have thought about it at some point in our lives. It touches all the social strata, the highest and the lowest, all races, all genders, all cultures, and all age groups.

- There were approximately **42,773 known deaths** by suicide in the U.S. in 2014.[11]
- There are approximately 25 suicide attempts for every one completion.[35]
- The World Health Organization estimates approximately **one million deaths** by suicide annually, globally.[9]
- Women attempt three times more than men. Men have four times more completions.[11]
- The suicide rate is highest among middle-aged white males.[11]
- Approximately 50% of suicides are committed with a firearm.[11]
- Highest rates: 65+ age group followed by 15-24 year olds.[9]

MYTHS of Suicide

1. **If I discuss suicide with a caller, she or he is more likely to do it.**
   False: In reality, it will be a relief for this individual to talk about it with an accepting person. For thoughts about suicide to be eliminated, they must be discussed.

2. **People who talk about killing themselves rarely commit suicide.**
   False: Most people who attempt suicide give some verbal clue or warning as a cry for help. Many times we do not take it seriously because it may be too much for us to deal with or we think it is just a cry for attention.

3. **Only insane people commit suicide.**
    False: *Only a small percentage of suicides are considered psychotic. Most are normal people who are depressed, grieving, lonely, and feeling hopeless.*

SYMPTOMS OF THE SUICIDAL MIND

- **Hopelessness.**
- **Helplessness.**
- **Worthlessness.**
- Feelings of failure/shame.
- Guilt.
- Despair.
- Empty to the point of numb . . . dead inside.
- Preoccupation with death.
- Talking about suicide.
- Suddenly happier, calmer.
- Loss of interest in things one cares about.
- Making arrangements . . . getting one's affairs in order.
- Giving things away.
- Self-mutilation.
- Eating/sleeping changes.
- Alcohol/drug abuse.
- Isolation/withdrawal.
- Lack of future plans.
- Irritability/anger.
- Underestimates their successes.
- Recalls negative experiences.
- Thinking is constricted and rigid and options narrow dangerously.
- Risk taking.

The more of these symptoms a person manifests, the higher the risk of suicide.

WHY SUICIDE?

"Suicide is man asserting himself against
the world one last time." –Eckhart Tolle

First of all, this is not going to be a discussion of suicide bombers or political statements or even low serotonin levels in the brain. This will be an examination of the thoughts and beliefs of someone who wants to live but also wants to escape the suffering they are in. This is representative of most of the people who call the crisis line. For 99% of people that call, it is *emotional pain* they cannot deal with.

There are certain characteristics about people or events that can increase the probability of a suicide attempt. Prudent listeners learn to read between the lines when dealing with possible suicide risk in callers.

Risk Factors:

- Giving verbal hints.
- Recent loss/break up.
- Past attempts – 50-80% of those who commit suicide have previously attempted.
- Changes in school, work, status, finance.
- Alcohol and/or drug abuse.
- Chronically or terminally ill.
- Psychiatric illness or recent release from mental hospital.
- Isolation or lack of support.
- Sexual/Gender identity issues.
- Abuse victim/unstable family.
- Unplanned pregnancies.
- Depression.
- Anxiety/panic attacks – can lead to despair, hopelessness, social isolation.
- A situation that causes great humiliation or shame.
- Confrontations with the law.
- Temperament – impulsivity, aggression.
- A friend or member of the family who has committed suicide.
- Suddenly being upbeat after coming out of a long depression. Sometimes just having a solution (even if it is to kill oneself) takes all the pressure off.

But these are not causes, they are risk factors. Many people have these experiences and do not contemplate suicide. So why some and not others?

It is an interesting phenomenon that many people in our culture believe that our number one motivation – our deepest drive is to survive. Then why is it that so many choose to kill themselves, voluntarily choosing to *not survive* anymore?

Is there a deeper motivation? A more important need that is not being fulfilled? What is it? Is it Love? Purpose? Freedom? Connectedness?

LOVE

*"The salvation of man is through love and
in love." –Viktor E. Frankl*

Is it love? The less we love ourselves and the more we feel unloved by others, the more we live in a world feeling scared, alone, unsafe and worthless. Love keeps us from destroying ourselves. Love will keep a family together. And love prevents societies from self-destructing.

Where there is no love, there is fear and shame. Shame feels empty and lacking so we strive to fill these holes with things outside of ourselves, like jobs, accomplishments, degrees, and relationships, in order to feel better, more safe and secure, more accepted and loved. But we become attached to those things, relying on them to bring us this love. So when suddenly we perceive a threat of it being taken away, we become fearful and even angry. And when it does get taken away, if feels like we are losing a part of ourselves, and all that approval and love we had are gone, leaving nothing but the hate and shame exposed.

Sometimes the loss and shame are so overwhelming that the fear takes over, limiting our reasoning ability. We begin to feel trapped in a self made prison, losing hope of ever escaping this pain, unable to tolerate ourselves anymore. We may not have learned to cope with loss and disappointment. And we haven't learned one of the deeper truths in life – **that our love and acceptance can only be found within.** And it can be found at any time by any one.

Love is the energy of life. It is the unseen bond that keeps us healthy, connected, and happy. When we do not feel love and we believe we never will, life suddenly does not seem worth living. Survival becomes meaningless.

PURPOSE

*"He who has a why to live can bear
with almost any how." –Nietzsche*

Most of our lives we strive and strive to gain love and acceptance from others. But we are motivated to look on the outside for it. When we get it, we try and hold on to it for dear life. It makes us feel more safe. After a while we might even believe we cannot *survive* without it. Pleasing our parents, living up to society's expectations, seeking status, wealth, accomplishments, doing things we really do not want to do, all to win other people's approval and love – this becomes our unconscious purpose in life.

And that is fine, but what happens if we feel like we do not fit in? What happens when attempt after attempt doesn't result in the permanent acceptance and safety we desire? When it constantly feels like it is not enough? Disappointment after disappointment,

156

leading to a feeling of helplessness. We begin to believe that it is because of who we are (we are worthless, defective, unlovable, etc) at our core. Shame. We then may lose hope of getting rid of these intolerable feelings and of ever attaining love, acceptance, safety. And without hope, there is no energy to keep going, there is no reason to continue on.

> *"If Man did not believe that he must live for something,*
> *he would not live at all." –Leo Tolstoy*

The impulse to actualize our potential is within us all. And it is first and foremost an inner journey. A realization that love and acceptance are within. Love is who we are at our core. Anything inside of us that tells us any different is conditioning we received from others who don't yet know who they are.

Depression and suicidal thoughts are often feedback that our strategies to experience love, freedom, and safety are not working anymore. That we are looking in the wrong direction.

FREEDOM

> *"All human motivation is toward greater freedom."*

People want freedom. We do not want to be told what to do or feel controlled by the whims of society's expectations. That feels like pressure. It also feels like prison. We will feel resentful, angry, rebellious, even violent, when we perceive our freedom is being suppressed. But, if the only coping skills we have learned keep us feeling trapped, we will begin to feel helpless, hopeless, and powerless. And then, our last attempt at freedom becomes a desperate cry for liberation from the despair of life itself.

There is no freedom when we have attached our happiness or approval to something outside of ourselves (another person, a job, status, etc.). Deep down we believe that we will be less happy without it. But in this material world, the fact is, *nothing lasts*. One day it will be gone. When we attach our happiness to something outside of ourselves we give our power away. We will feel anxious about losing it and resentful and angry about not feeling in control.

But freedom can also be scary. It entails risk. The risk of stepping into the unknown. So many of us stay in our known misery rather than take this risk, believing that trying something new might bring even more pain. We may fear getting our hopes up just to fail and be let down once again.

Most of us are not comfortable with ourselves as we are. So we project ourselves into the future, believing it is there that happiness will occur, or into the past to moments when we felt better. But when we look into our past and see only pain and our belief is that the future will hold nothing but the same, then we feel trapped. Nowhere to go. Nowhere to escape to. Except to escape life altogether.

> *"The last of human freedoms is the ability to choose*
> *one's attitude in a given set of circumstances."* –*Viktor E. Frankl*

Freedom is the awareness that we always have a choice – with the thoughts we pay attention to, the attitudes we hold, the way we hold ourselves, and with our behaviors. Freedom is knowing that our power and control resides within ourselves with these choices. Freedom and self-responsibility are very closely linked.

CONNECTEDNESS

> *"We are like islands in the sea . . . separate on the surface,*
> *but connected in the deep."* –*William James*

Most people who feel stuck in a suicidal mindset are identifying completely with their egos (our constructed/conditioned sense of self), trapped in its comparing, lacking, inferior prison of self-conscious fear and shame. Our identity is wrapped up in believing we *are* lazy, stupid, ugly, bad, etc., and we are *always* going to be that way.

Most mystics, philosophers, and great thinkers believe that in order to experience love, freedom, purpose, and connectedness, we must take a higher, wider, deeper perspective of who we are. Most of us believe ourselves to be only our personality, or our body, or the roles we play. But these things change all the time. Our true Self, our essence, that which is aware of all that changes – is changeless, eternal, and all loving.

This essence is what connects all human beings. It is what connects the entire universe.

> *"The experience of separateness arouses anxiety;*
> *it is, indeed, the source of all anxiety."* –*Erich Fromm*

When we feel connected, knowing everything we think and do affects the whole, we gain a sense of power. We also know that what we do to others we do to ourselves because we are part of that whole. So we want to help others because that means helping ourselves. Why do you think it feels so good to help people?

When we change this sense of identity, we gain a new sense of freedom and inner power and control. We no longer feel like a victim of our own mind and personality. How we express ourselves and how we respond in any situation becomes our choice. We realize it was the judgments that created the fear and the false barriers between people.

When we know we are whole and connected to this whole, fear dissipates, a load lifts off us, and peace and joy move in.

"The cry for escape – the cry for death – is really a cry to reinterpret how one sees themselves and the world. A psychological death to their old identity. And a rebirth to a new pattern of being and thinking." –James Hillman

Taking the suicide call:

"No one keeps anyone else alive. Our job is to buy time in the hope that the help we provide will allow the person to reconsider and perhaps come to a different decision."

Of all the emotionally loaded situations faced by crisis workers, suicide is the most frightening. The urgent life and death nature of suicide brings out the rescuer in all of us. We often harbor the belief that we can be responsible for saving the suicide. We also harbor the terrifying belief that we may push the person "over the edge" and become responsible for the death. It is true you might be their last hope, but whatever their decision it is <u>NEVER your responsibility</u>. Their actions are *their* responsibility. There is no such thing as *"I blew it and that's why he's dead,"* or *"It is my fault."* Never. We offer our help but ultimately it is their decision to make. We do the best we can.

If a person comes to us because they are thinking of trying drugs and we advise against it, letting them know all the possible consequences, providing them information, and then they do the drugs anyway, that was their decision. It is not our fault or responsibility. We did the best we could.

This perspective will not reduce our motivation to help. If anything, it *will* reduce our anxiety, getting us out of our own head and issues, so we can be clear minded and more able to help.

We cannot fix all of their problems. We will not cause them to be suddenly happy forever. We are here TO GET THEM THROUGH THE NIGHT. Most listeners will have some fear of not being able to do this. You can! Follow the guidelines, stay calm and you will handle it fine. Once you get through the call, it can be quite exhilarating.

There are many different suicidal situations we may have to deal with and we will go through them all. But the first thing to work on is staying calm. Before picking up any phone call it helps to take a deep breath and create an intention or mantra you can say to yourself to get into a calm, focused state of mind. It often settles a caller in a confused state of mind to hear a very calm yet concerned voice on the other end.

Responding to a suicidal caller can be intimidating for a listener and understandably a source of personal stress. The crisis worker is encouraged to seek and accept emotional support from fellow listeners and Supervisors, as well as therapists.

Example 1: *John hints at killing himself during the call . . .*

Hints could mean: *"None of this seems worth it anymore. I won't be around next week." "There is no meaning to any of this. Why bother?"* It could be anything. The key is to pick up on the hint and go with your intuition and <u>*ask him directly*</u>:

> ***"Are you thinking of killing yourself, John?"***
> ***"It sounds as if suicide is on your mind."***

Asking directly does not make it more likely to happen. It actually works the opposite way. People cry out with these indirect hints, hoping someone will ask. They want to talk about their pain because talking about it often relieves them of the emotional pressure inside. You may be scared to ask, but trust your gut feeling and do it anyway. If he is not thinking of it, he will just say he is not. It is important that we communicate in a calm manner that we are not afraid to talk about suicide.

If he *is* thinking of suicide, we want to determine how serious the *risk* is right now. So the next thing we must ask is:

> ***"Do you have a plan?"***

If yes, he does have a plan, then obviously he is pretty serious about it.

Now we want to find out **more about the plan.**

> ***"What is your plan?"***
> ***"When will you carry it out?"***
> ***"Where?"***
> ***"Have you bought the means?"***

Get all the details.

Check safety

> *"Where are you right now?"*
> *"Is there anyone else there with you?"*
> *"Do you feel safe?"*
> *"Have you been taking anything? Drinking? Drugs?"*

Check the **history of suicide** in their life.

> *"Have you ever attempted to kill yourself before?"*

"Do you have any friends or family members who have attempted suicide?"

Check their **support system**.

"Have you told anyone else about your intentions/feelings?"
"Who do you talk to when you are down?"
"How does your friends or family respond to your concerns?"

How much **control** does the person have?

"Can anyone or anything stop you?"
"What has been stopping you?"
"What made you call for help?"

If we gently ask the caller <u>why they have stayed alive thus far</u>, we many learn something about what he values and wants to live for.

We want to get the caller to talk about their pain. LISTEN, LISTEN, LISTEN. Having no one to listen to is probably a major cause of why they are feeling this way in the first place. Avoid dealing with a suicidal caller's feelings and they may end up feeling more alone and beyond help. A person really cannot think straight unless their emotions are dealt with first.

Validate and normalize their feelings and **empathize with the pain, suffering,** and pressure they feel. Ask open-ended questions to gain information about the circumstances that have led him to seriously contemplate taking his own life.

"How long have you been feeling this way?"
"Was there something that triggered these feelings?"

We want the caller to talk in great detail about the pain in his life. To open up about the things that he has tried, the things that have failed, the people he has turned to, the disappointments in his life, the desperation that he lives with.

"Sounds like you have high expectations for yourself."
"Sounds like you put a lot of pressure on yourself."
"Do you feel pressured by anyone?"
"Tell me about it."

Constricted thinking makes him believe that suicide is his only available option to deal with this pain. We want to open up the lens on his thinking viewfinder. Show him that there are other possibilities. Come up with all the possibilities you and he can think of, then have him list all the choices and rank them. *We must widen their blinders from a hopeless viewpoint to one that includes other possibilities.*

More than likely, he will be feeling **powerless** and using a lot of victim-like words such as, *"won't, can't, have to, must, never, always,"* as well as seeing everything in black and white terms. Encourage and assist him to see the shades of grey.

Perception Check throughout the call while **Reflecting** his feelings back so that he can begin to connect his thoughts and feelings. Doing this will let him know that we are listening and that we understand.

Be patient. Stay positive.

This is the one instance when we *can* give advice:

> **"I don't think you should kill yourself."**
> **"What would it take to keep you alive?"**

Example 2: *John is thinking of killing himself. He has a gun in his hand.*

In this situation or any situation where the person has the means (guns, pills, blade, on a ledge, driving a car, head in a noose, etc.) our first step is to **get them away from the means.** This is a very precarious situation and the last thing we want to have happen is to hear the death over the phone. We want to put some space between the person, his means, and his immediate thoughts of taking his life.

> **"Please place the gun down, John."**
>
> *"In order for me to talk to you, you have to **first put the gun down**. It's not going anywhere, and I really want to help you."*
>
> *"I think you called tonight for a reason, let's talk about it. But in order to do that please put the gun down for me."*

Then ask him to go into another room.

> **"Could you please go into another room?"**
> *"It would make me more comfortable. You can come back in after we speak."*

If he is driving a car, get him to pull over and turn off the engine.
With ledges, get him to back away and go inside if it is possible.
Get him away from the means while you are speaking with him <u>and keep checking throughout the call</u>.

If he refuses to do so, get curious about what his concerns are.

> *"If you were to back away, what is your concern would happen?"*

Be creative. And if still no, then we warn him that we will be forced to hang up. **And then we will hang up.** This sounds cruel, but we do not want to hear him die.

> *"**I'm going to hang up now**. I really hope you don't kill yourself, and I'm here to help when you're ready to put the gun down and talk with me."*

Example 3: *John has a gun and he begins counting down 10-9-8, threatening to kill himself.*

Maybe he is even demanding we do something in order to get him to stop. This is manipulation. We can ask him to stop and even plead that we want to help, but if he does not stop the countdown, we <u>must</u> hang up the phone before he reaches a low number.

Example 4: *John has ingested a lethal amount of pills or drugs . . .*

We first want to *gather information* – his name and address – so we can send help. We work under the assumption that when a person in this situation calls us they want help. Plead with him for information if you have to. Be creative.

If he is slurring or becoming incoherent, *keep him focused*. Say his name sharply and loudly to snap him to. Ask him for information directly and sharply, over and over if you have to. **Shout if necessary**. Do not give up. Be creative.

Get information and keep him on the phone and alert until the help arrives. Ask him short direct questions in succession. Safety questions and personal information,

> *"John, what did you take!?"*
> *"How much, John!?"*
> *"How long ago!?"*
> *"John, Is there anyone else there!?"*
> *"John, where are you!?"*
> *"John, I need you to stay with me here. Listen to my voice, John!"*
> *"John, what is your address!? Your phone number?"*

Get him to sit up. Do not have him stand up because he could fall down and hurt himself.

Example 5: *A repeat caller has been mentioning suicide on and off for a long time.*

<u>Every threat of suicide is taken seriously</u>, even if they have said it a thousand times and not attempted. You never know. If we believe they are now using these threats for attention, we can gently confront them on this . . .

> *"It sounds as if you are receiving attention every time you mention suicide? Do you want to talk about that? This is understandable given that you feel no one cares about you or listens to you."*

Example 6: *John has a friend who is threatening suicide and does not know what to do.*

In this situation our task is to help John to help the other person. **Listen** to him and **Validate** his feelings of *helplessness and powerlessness.* It is important to make sure we help him get to a calmer state before moving ahead, then talk to him about how to help. Where is that person now? Do they have a plan? When? Where? Tell him to stay positive even if the friend becomes angry with him. Find him some hope.

Make sure to let him know that he is not responsible for his friend's actions. All he can do is help. <u>Tell him not to leave this person alone.</u> Get other friends and family involved (unless he really hates his family.) Remove any means or sharp objects from his environment. Listen, empathize, and ask him about his pain. Teach him as much as you possibly can over the phone. Give him our number and ask him to encourage the friend to call us or another suicide hotline. Encourage him to call us back if necessary.

If we get the feeling that the caller may be talking about himself and not really a friend, we can gently confront him on this.

> *"I'm wondering if this friend you are talking about is really you. Is this true, John?"*

If it is not true, just **buy it back** and continue on as before. If he *is* really talking about himself, we can focus the call directly on him now.

What not to say to a suicidal caller:

- *"Things will get better."* (because things may not)
- *"Life is worth living."* (invalidating the caller's reality)

- *"Time heals all wounds."* (they feel they have no time left. And it doesn't always.)
- *"It isn't that bad."* (invalidating the caller's reality).
- Do not argue whether suicide is wrong or right.

Before closing the call, always make **a contract** with the caller:

> *"Okay John, I'm really glad you called tonight and **I want you to promise me that you are not going to kill yourself tonight,** and that you will call the therapist tomorrow first thing."*

This is very important. We are not going to end the call with the person until we get that contract from them. It really could save their life. *Get them to promise,* and when they do, tell them they can call us back any time.

> *"Don't hesitate to call us back anytime, John."*

FINDING HOPE

Our obligation is to do whatever it takes to help this person reconsider and make the choice not to commit suicide.

Let them know that there *is* a way out of this. Discovering things that make him feel good, hopeful, and give his life purpose is the key.

> *"Do you have any goals? Any dreams?"*
> *"Is there anything you are interested in?"*
> *"If you could start all over again, with no pressure, and the freedom to do or be anything, what would you do? What would you like to be like?"*

Are there any significant others in their life? Spouse? Family? Kids? Friends? Pets? Any groups or organizations they go to? Church? Therapy? Support groups? School? **Open up their narrow view of their life and resources.**

Once something is found that seems to spark the caller, explore it fully, assisting the caller in seeing it as something meaningful to live for.

Help them envision a future where they will feel better. One where they are helping others deal with this similar problem. Inform them that there are people out there, including us, to help them as they take steps toward feeling better about themselves and life.

Let them know that it is possible and indeed normal to hold opposing thoughts in one's mind. This can sometimes reduce their intolerance for these conflicting forces within, and help them to become aware of the motivations of both.[3]

"It sounds like you have two voices in your head. One that wants to end your pain and escape this misery somehow and another voice that still wants to live and love and somehow find some happiness. I would like to hear more of what both voices have to say."

This is a good time for personal experiences if we have any. Do not let the call become about us. But if we have an experience that we believe will help normalize their feelings and give them hope for positive change, then by all means share it.

Encourage them to find their power in the situation, to observe the choices they have made, and how they may have needed to create this situation to learn more about themselves.

Be creative. Be patient. Don't give up.

The crisis of suicide is often a transformational life occurrence, with the immediate opportunity to open up to our spiritual side. If we are familiar with this, we can talk about it. Shakti Gawain illustrates this nicely in her book *Living in the Light*.

"Most of us have spent many years looking outside of ourselves, trying to find fulfillment in the world of form. Eventually we realize that it's not working: no matter what we do in the world, we don't find happiness. In frustration and hopelessness, we give up. It feels like hitting bottom. It is a time of ego death, when the body/mind form recognizes the hopelessness of trying to live this way and surrenders its fight. It would rather die than keep trying. But the darkest hour is truly just before the dawn. When we finally give up the struggle to find fulfillment "out there, we have nowhere to go but within. It is at this moment of total surrender that the light begins to dawn. We expect to hit bottom, but instead we fall through a trap door into a bright new world. We've discovered the world of our spirit." [36]

Survivors of Suicide

People who succeed in taking their own life pass their pain on to the loved ones they leave behind. Survivors of suicide experience most of the normal grief reactions like *sadness, anger, and depression*, as well as some particular feelings:

- Powerful, long lasting **guilt.**

An angry suicide note, not taking warning signs seriously, and any unresolved issues with the deceased can increase the guilt and complicate the grief process.

> *"If only I would have taken her seriously."*
> *"If only I hadn't argued with her."*

- Trying to figure out **what went wrong** and what they could have been done differently or better.
- Feeling very **alone in their pain**, feeling no one understands.
    > There is a stigma associated with suicide in our culture and especially in our religions. The family often gets blamed for the death so they do not tell the truth or they try to cover it up.
- A **need to blame** someone as a means to make sense of this event.
- **Shock and denial.** Sometimes refusing to admit the death was a suicide.
- **Nightmares** or reliving the experience.
    > The death is often violent and usually occurs at home. Often the family finds the body or the suicide happens in front of them.

Resources and Referrals

While a call to the line may have an immediate, calming effect, our goal should be to refer this caller to an agency or private practitioner who will provide long term assistance.

- Support groups are extremely helpful for many.
- Counseling is recommended for all people thinking of suicide.
- Book referrals to help people understand themselves better (see bibliography).
- Exploring the internet for information or support.
- Calling other hotlines if we are not available.

Empathy and Suicide

> ***"As we acknowledge our own vulnerability and accept vulnerability in others, we make the world easier to live in for all of us."***

<u>**Journal on**</u> any times you have felt down, alone, depressed, suicidal. How did you cope? What would you have wanted from others during this time? What kind of pressure and expectations were you feeling?

Notice your feelings of powerlessness when helping a caller who is thinking of suicide. Sometimes nothing we do seems to be helping or making a difference. We cannot save people or rescue them. We can only do the best we can to help them see they have other choices. Ultimately is it their decision and responsibility whether they live or die.

Empathize with a person on the brink of suicide. Think about all of their feelings – the incredible aloneness, the despair, the hate toward themselves and the world, feeling like they cannot talk to anyone and that no one cares. How would it be to feel that hopeless and helpless? What would you want from someone if you were feeling this way?

Be aware

- That every human being wants to love and be loved.

- Every human being is doing the best they can, given their life circumstances and level of self-awareness to cope and find happiness.

- All human beings are connected to each other. What each of us thinks and does affects the whole. Everyone counts and everyone is integral to the whole.

EMPATHY DEVELOPMENT

Releasing Judgments
Exercise #5

Releasing judgments reduces conflict and helps mankind to evolve.

"Empathy creates the invisible connections that hold us together, one human to another, neighborhood to village, community to country, nation to planet. With the connectedness that empathy engenders, the world itself becomes a less frightening place. A sense of belonging replaces loneliness, strangers appear less strange, defenses seem less necessary, and hope replaces hopelessness. Doubts give way to faith, resentments fade, and our hearts, once closed by fear and pain, open up to the possibility of forgiveness." –Power of Empathy

The world seems to be changing at an ever increasing rate and our abilities to adapt are being put to the test. From a systems perspective, it appears we are being pushed to a threshold where we are forced to find our center, our core, in order to cope.

This center, this core, is where the peace, love, compassion, acceptance, freedom, wisdom, and joy that we have been searching for reside. It is within us. And it begins by cultivating another one of its qualities – curiosity.

Mindfulness exercises have been shown to develop the ability to access our curious observer – the presence within us that is aware and can non-judgmentally notice and be with all of the sensations, emotions, thoughts, desires, and memories that come and go. It assists us with catching our judgments and letting them pass. It helps us with noticing and being with the pain in others without needing to judge or fix. It is both wise and compassionate.

"All man's miseries derive from not being able
to sit quietly in a room alone." –Blaise Pascal

Here is a mindfulness exercise to try out:

1. Body Scan.

Lie down in a comfortable place where it is quiet. You can use headphones with soft music to block out distractions if you like. Begin by taking a few deep breaths. Then focus the spotlight of your awareness into your feet. Notice everything you can about how your feet feel – the sensations, tension, soreness, etc. Do your feet feel relaxed and open or are they fidgety? Is it hard to connect with sensations in your feet? Notice that too. Let whatever shows up be okay.

Next move your awareness up to your shins and calves and do the same noticing. One part at a time, moving up the body (thighs, hamstrings, hips, pelvis, lower-mid-upper back, abdomen, heartspace, upper chest, shoulders, upper arms, forearms, hands, neck, each part of the face and head).

Take time to notice each body part, practicing maintaining your focus there, and deepening your ability to notice and be with all of the different sensations and feelings.

When you have a thought, just notice it, let it pass, and move back into your body awareness.

If you notice an eager or impatient part of you that has an agenda to do it well or get rid of feelings or to be more relaxed, ask that part to step back. That is not the intention. The intention is to build your curious observer and strengthen the muscle of being able to notice, accept, and be with whatever shows up within, even if doesn't feel pleasant.

This practice can be much easier to do when it is guided. See the EmpathyWorks website at www.empathyworks.net to access guided mindfulness exercises.

Burnout and Support for Listeners

Particularly in crisis calls, it can be difficult to let go of the call when it is over. "Heavier" calls have a tendency to stick with us and can be very draining. It is important to talk about these feelings. We cannot place enough stress on the fact that the staff are here to help us avoid burnout, as well as to address our concerns.[5]

Some symptoms of burnout include feeling abused, used, or angry and frustrated with repeat callers.

When people don't change the way we want them to in the time we want them to, we can become frustrated, jaded, and cynical. This can lead to burnout and negativity and can be a signal that it is time to explore and heal some of our personal judgments. We may also feel resentful from time to time when our care for others severely outweighs our care and time for ourselves.

If you find yourself becoming cynical or pessimistic or even judgmental toward callers – or even humans in general – it may be time to look within at your own feelings of helplessness, your own self-judgments of being incompetent and selfish, and your own need to fix, change, rescue, or transform others.

Some professionals believe burnout is a sign that we are being too empathic and we need to reduce our empathy. This is inaccurate. More empathy is the answer. A different level of empathy. The burnout is a signal that we have our own material that is interfering with our ability to help. The emotional issues in others touches upon the unresolved material within us. This is not bad. It is what shows up at a stage of empathy development where we are able to feel and attune to others at a very high and deep level. But empathy keeps growing and now we must work on and resolve some of our own inner obstacles in order to serve people at an even higher level, and without the burnout.

The mindfulness, empathy, and judgment exercises located within this book and on the EmpathyWorks website can provide some effective support.

At the same time, talk with your shift partner or supervisor, take some time off, practice self-care, seek out a therapist, and thank yourself for being of service to others.

ETHICS AND CONFIDENTIALITY

Here are some general guidelines regarding ethics and confidentiality for crisis lines. Be sure to be informed of any specific rules and policies for the organization you are affiliated with.

- All information disclosed on a crisis line is strictly confidential within the crisis line. Calls and callers are not to be discussed outside of the organization.

- Information regarding members of the crisis line (i.e. shift times, personal information) is not to be disclosed to any non-crisis line member.

- Policies and information (rules, meeting places and times, room location, etc.) are strictly confidential.

- Outside contact with a caller is prohibited.

- Repeat relationships with callers is discouraged. (i.e. *"You can call me next Thursday at 6 p.m."*).

- Always be respectful, truthful, and authentic with callers.

- Revealing personal information is discouraged unless relevant to normalizing a caller's experience in order to gain rapport, trust, or give hope.

- Be Professional. Everything we do is for the caller's benefit. When taking a call, it is not the time to talk about our own issues and feelings. It also means recognizing our own limitations and referring callers to appropriate sources of factual information.

BE THE CHANGE

*"As human beings, our greatness lies not so much in being able
to remake the world . . . as in being able to remake ourselves."*
    –Mahatma Gandhi

Our training affords us the opportunity to learn to take others' perspectives and widen and deepen our own perspectives and worldviews. Take the time to go back and work on any exercises you may have skipped over. Examining our judgments and deepening our empathy are the foundations to being able to assist people in their growth and development.

*"Everyone thinks of changing the world,
    but no one thinks of changing himself."* *–Leo Tolstoy*

To reduce conflict in this world, we must also reduce the conflict within ourselves. Be a model for the kind of change you want to see. Use these new ways of communicating in your day-to-day life and not just on the crisis line.

The world needs us now to start caring. Each of us has an immense power to make a difference.

ABOUT THE AUTHOR

Kurt Christiansen is a licensed clinical psychologist and trauma specialist with over 18 years of experience working with people in crisis as well as training professionals and non-professionals in crisis intervention, counseling skills, and empathy development.

For more information, go to www.EmpathyWorks.net

RECOMMENDED READINGS

Empathy, Judgment, Shame, and Healing
- Healing the Shame that Binds You – John Bradshaw
- Meeting the Shadow – Connie Zweig and Jeremiah Abrams
- The Dark Side of Light Chasers – Debbie Ford
- Inward and Upward – Kurt Christiansen
- Knowing Your Shadow – Robert Augustus Masters
- Self Therapy – Jay Earley
- The Empathic Civilization – Jeremy Rifkin
- ShadowLight – Keith Witt
- A New Earth – Eckhart Tolle
- Conscious Evolution – Barbara Marx Hubbard
- Conversations with God – Neale Donald Walsch
- No Boundary – Ken Wilber
- Your Sacred Self – Wayne Dyer
- Living in the Light – Shakti Gawain
- The Compassionate Presence – Stephen R. Schwartz
- The Gifts of Imperfection – Brene Brown
- Mindsight – Daniel J. Siegel
- Forgiveness – Robin Casarjian
- Loveability – Robert Holden
- How to Love Yourself When You Don't Know How – Jacqui Bishop and Mary Grunte
- Healing Your Emotional Self – Beverly Engel
- Radical Forgiveness – Colin C. Tipping
- How Can I Help – Ram Dass and Paul Gorman
- Fried – Joan Borysenko
- Embracing Your Inner Critic – Hal Stone and Sidra Stone
- Buddha's Brain: The Practical Neuroscience of Happiness, Love, and Wisdom – Rick Hanson
- Reclaiming the Inner Child – Jeremiah Abrams

Death and Dying
- Grace and Grit – Ken Wilber
- Who Dies – Stephen Levine
- No Death, No Fear – Thich Nhat Hanh
- The Grief Recovery Handbook – John W. James & Russel Friedman

Domestic Violence and Sexual Assault
- The Abusive Personality – Donald G. Dutton
- The Battered Woman – Lenore Walker

- The Batterer – Donald G. Dutton
- Dangerous Relationships – Noelle Nelson
- From Generation to Generation – Understanding Sexual Attraction to Children – Anne Stirling Hastings
- It Wasn't Your Fault – Beverly Engel
- The Emotionally Abusive Relationship – Beverly Engel
- Legacy of the Heart: The Spiritual Advantages of a Painful Childhood – Wayne Muller
- The Courage to Heal – Ellen Bass & Laura Davies

Addiction

- Loosening the Grip: Handbook of Alcohol Information – Jean Kinney
- Addiction & Grace – Gerald G. May
- The Heart of Addiction – Lance Dodes
- Power vs. Force – David R. Hawkins
- The Healing Journey Through Addiction – Phil Rich and Stuart A. Copans
- An Internal Family Systems Guide to Recovery From Eating Disorders – Amy Yandel Grabowski
- Life Without Ed: How One Woman Declared Independence from Her Eating Disorder and How You Can Too – Jenni Schaefer

Relationships and Communication

- Facing Co-Dependency – Pia Melody
- Creating Harmonious Relationships – Andrew LeCompte
- Non-Violent Communication – Marshall B. Rosenberg
- Taking Responsibility – Nathaniel Branden
- The Relationship Cure – John M. Gottman
- Conscious Loving – Gay Hendricks and Kathlyn Hendricks
- Social Intelligence – Daniel Goleman
- The Power of Empathy – Arthur P. Ciaramicoli and Katherine Ketcham
- The Science of Parenting – Margot Sunderland
- Emotional Intimacy – Robert Augustus Masters
- Creating Harmonious Relationships – Andrew LeCompte

Trauma

- The Body Keeps the Score – Bessel A. van der Kolk
- It Didn't Start with You – Mark Wolynn
- In an Unspoken Voice – Peter A. Levine

Suicide and Depression

- Man's Search for Meaning – Victor E. Frankl
- Suicide and the Soul – James Hillman
- The Mindful Way Through Depression – Mark Williams, John Teasdale, Zindel Segal, and Jon Kabat-Zinn

REFERENCES

[1] Kennedy, Eugene and Charles, Sara C., M.D. 1990. On Becoming a Counselor. New York: The Crossroad Publishing Co.

[2] LeCompte, Andrew. 2000. Creating Harmonious Relationships - A practical guide to the Power of True Empathy. Portsmouth, NH: Atlantic Books.

[3] Lester, David. 2002. Crisis Intervention and Counseling by Telephone. Springfield, Illinois: Charles C. Thomas Publisher LTD.

[4] Ciaramicoli, Arthur P, Ed.D., PhD and Katherine Ketcham. 2000. The Power of Empathy. New York: Penguin Putnam Inc.

[5] Meier, Sue and Kara Fitzpatrick. CSUN HelpLine Manual.

[6] Roberts, Albert R. 1990. Crisis Intervention Handbook. Belmont, CA: Wadsworth Publishing CO.

[7] Hammond, D. Corydon, Dean H. Hepworth and Veon G. Smith. 2002. Improving Therapeutic Communication. San Francisco: Jossey-Bass.

[8] Statistics from National Institute of Mental Health (2015).

[9] Statistics from World Health Organization (2017).

[10] Statistics from National Mental Health Association (NMHA) study reported in *MSNBC Health Today,* March 10, 2004.

[11] Statistics from The Centers for Disease Control and Prevention (2016).

[12] James, John W., and Russel Friedman. 1998. The Grief Recovery Handbook. New York: HarperCollins.

[13] Statistics from UNAIDS (2016).

[14] Haas, Herman, and Rodgers (2014). Suicide Attempts among Transgender and Gender Non-Conforming Adults: Finding of the National Transgender Discrimination Survey. American Foundation for Suicide Prevention and The Williams Institute. https://williamsinstitute.law.ucla.edu/wp-content/uploads/AFSP-Williams-Suicide-Report-Final.pdf

[15] Dodes, Lance, M.D. 2002. The Heart of Addiction. New York: HarperCollins.

[16] Gawain, Shakti. 1989. Return to the Garden. Mill Valley, CA: Nataraj Publishing.

[17] Hawkins, David R., M.D., Ph.D. 1995. Power vs. Force. Carlsbad, CA: Hay House.

[18] Greenwald, Barry, Ph.D., Article in CSUN HelpLine Manual - Crisis Section (2000).

[19] Colquhoun, Karen. 2001. The INFO LINE Crisis Handbook. San Gabriel. CA: INFO LINE.

[20] Kanel, Kristi. 1999. A Guide to Crisis Intervention. Pacific Grove, CA: Brooks/Cole Publishing Company.

[21] Plonski, John. 2008. Working *with* Difficult Interactions. Covenant House International.

[22] Child Maltreatment Report. 2015. Data gathered by Child Protective Services agencies.

[23] Statistics from www.yesican.org

[24] Statistics from www.Childhelp.org

[25] National Coalition to Prevent Child Sexual Abuse and Exploitation. (2012). National Plan to Prevent the Sexual Abuse and Exploitation of Children.

[26] Statistics from www.Avert.org

[27] Bass, Ellen and Laura Davis. 1988. The Courage to Heal. New York: Harper&Row.

[28] Kaufman, Gershen. Shame: The Power of Caring. Cambridge, Mass.: Schenkman Books.

[29] Rogers, Carl. 1961. On Becoming a Person: A Therapist's View of Psychotherapy. Boston: Houghton Mifflin Company.

[30] Statistics from the National Coalition Against Domestic Violence (NACDV).

[31] Wilson, K.J., Ed.D. 1997. When Violence Begins at Home. Alameda, Ca: Hunter House Publishers.

[32] Walker, Lenore E. 1979. The Battered Woman. New York: HarperPerennial.

[33] Department of Justice, Office of Justice Programs, Bureau of Justice Statistics, National Crime Victimization Survey, 2010-2014 (2015).

[33] Statistics from National Sexual Violence Resource Center.

[34] Valley Trauma Center. Common Misconceptions About Rape and Sexual Assault.

[35] Statistics from http://www.suicidology.org

[35] Statistics from The American Foundation for Suicide Prevention. (formerly L)

[36] Gawain, Shakti. 1986. Living in the Light. New York: Bantam Books.